THE WESTERN FRONTIER LIBRARY

(Complete list on pages 116–18)

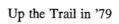
Up the Trail in '79

Up the Trail
in '79

By Baylis John Fletcher

EDITED AND WITH AN INTRODUCTION BY

Wayne Gard

UNIVERSITY OF OKLAHOMA PRESS

NORMAN

34620

The paper on which this book is printed bears the water-mark of the University of Oklahoma Press and is designed for an effective life of at least three hundred years.

Library of Congress Catalog Card Number: 67–64460

Copyright February, March, April, May, 1966, by *The Cattleman.* Assigned 1967 to the University of Oklahoma Press. New edition copyright 1968 by the University of Oklahoma Press, Publishing Division of the University. Composed and printed at Norman, Oklahoma, U.S.A., by the University of Oklahoma Press. First printing.

Foreword

OF THE THOUSANDS of rugged Texas cowmen who rode up the Chisholm and other trails with herds of Longhorn cattle, most died without setting down their experiences on paper. So scarce are firsthand trail-drive accounts which are both authentic and detailed that the finding of any new one is something of a Texana discovery.

Thus I was pleased when, in 1965, Dick Wilson, editor of *The Cattleman*, wrote that he had received such a narrative and asked me to come over to Fort Worth to see it. This was the chronicle of Baylis John Fletcher, who, as a young cowboy, had helped to point a herd to Kansas and on to Wyoming in 1879, and who died in 1912.

This account, which had been gathering dust for many years, seemed important enough to warrant not only its publication in four installments in *The Cattleman*, which was done in February–May, 1966, but also its appearance in a book. I wrote to the author's son, Roddy W. Fletcher of Giddings, Texas, and arranged with him for editing the manuscript for book publication. He suggested the inclusion of several short pieces on related frontier subjects which his father had written for various periodicals.

The short sketches, like the trail narrative, are true accounts except that in "The Regulators" the son has struck out the name of the slave-stealer and changed the name of the mob leader.

In place of footnotes it has seemed preferable in this case to insert in the text a number of short explanatory and interpretive passages. Since these are enclosed with brackets, they will not be confused with the Fletcher chronicle.

In editing the narrative, I have been helped by Roddy W. Fletcher, who provided biographical information about his father, and by Mrs. Susie Snyder Pace of Dallas, who gave information about her father, Captain Thomas S. Snyder, owner of the cattle that Baylis Fletcher helped to trail north.

Further help came from Miss Jamie Kate Byrne, who looked up cattle-brand registrations in the county brand book at Victoria, Texas, and from librarians and archivists in Dallas, Fort Worth, Austin, Topeka, and Denver.

WAYNE GARD

Dallas, Texas
January 3, 1968

Introduction

By WAYNE GARD

———————◆———————

BAYLIS JOHN FLETCHER's horseback trip up the Chisholm Trail with a herd of Longhorn cattle in 1879 was part of a gigantic trek that has stirred the American imagination. For three generations, cowmen have been reminiscing, and even singing, about the guiding of bawling herds over this winding route from the windswept plains of Texas to northern markets. Now, after a century, they see the trail firmly embedded in history.

For the frontier cowhand "on a ten-dollar horse and a forty-dollar saddle," the Chisholm Trail was something real. It wasn't just a solution to a marketing problem that ranchmen faced after the Civil War. It meant long hours in the saddle, through dust or rain. It spelled the perils of river crossings, of midnight stampedes, of raids by whooping Comanches. It was a road to high adventure.

I woke up one morning on the old Chisholm Trail,
Rope in my hand and a cow by the tail.

Feet in the stirrups and seat in the saddle,
I hung and rattled with them Longhorn cattle.

Back in 1867, when it took the imprint of its first herds,

the Chisholm Trail led through wild country. Streams were without bridges, and the Indian Territory was occupied by tribes who resented the intrusion of the Texas herds that ate much of their grass. But a new trail had to be blazed farther west than the old Shawnee Trail, on which drovers had run into serious trouble in Missouri and Kansas because their herds brought tick fever, which many called Texas fever.

The need for a new cattle market and a new trail, west of most of the farm settlements, was met by a young Illinois stock dealer, Joseph G. McCoy. In the summer of 1867, McCoy built shipping yards and a hotel in the frontier village of Abilene, in central Kansas, on the Union Pacific Railroad. He invited Texas ranchmen to bring their herds there and gave them directions for the route.

By mid-August, before the yards and hotel were completed, the first herds had arrived at Abilene. Most of them had come up the old Shawnee Trail and turned west along the southern border of Kansas. The first herd brought all the way up the new Chisholm Trail was one of 2,400 head that Colonel O. W. Wheeler and two associates had started in San Antonio. This outfit also had more than one hundred cow ponies and fifty-four Texas trail hands with Colt six-shooters and the new Henry repeating rifles to protect the cattle in the Indian Territory.

McCoy made his first shipment from Abilene on September 5. It filled twenty stockcars and was headed for Chicago. That night McCoy and his friends celebrated in a tent with feasting, toasting, and flowery speeches. From this small beginning, use of the new trail increased rapidly. An estimated 75,000 cattle were trailed to Abilene in 1868; 150,000 in 1869; 300,000 to Abilene and rival markets in 1870; and 600,000 to 700,000 in the peak year of 1871.

After the 1871 season, Abilene residents asked the Texas drovers to market their cattle elsewhere, since crime and vice were hurting the town. In the next three years, Ellsworth and Wichita divided most of the Texas trade. In 1876 a new and rival Western trail was opened through Fort Griffin to Dodge City. But some herds continued to tramp up the Chisholm Trail to the Cimarron River. From there they either were sold at Caldwell or, as in the case of the one which young Fletcher accompanied, were pointed northwest to Dodge.

Although railroads began to haul some Texas cattle north in the spring of 1873, much trailing continued. Not only were the railways unable to carry more than a fraction of the cattle, but trailing was much cheaper. By the mid-1880's, farmers and their fences had pushed westward to cut off the main trails. Trailing over long distances virtually ceased in the latter part of that decade.

The Chisholm and other trails had carried out of Texas nine to ten million cattle, making the greatest movement of domestic animals ever known. By taking eight-dollar steers to thirty-dollar markets, the trails had helped the Southwest to recover from the economic blows of the Civil War and to put cattle ranching on a stable basis. They also helped to stock northwestern ranges, supplied domestic and European food needs, and were a factor in the displacement of pork by beef as the chief meat item on American dinner tables.

Money from the sale of trail cattle enabled Texas ranchmen to buy and fence range land, put in wells and windmills, and upgrade their herds by the use of British bulls. The trails also spurred the growth of Chicago and Kansas City as centers for beef packing, encouraged the building of western railroads, and hastened the development of refrigerator cars and the canning of meat. In addition, travel up and down the trails helped to heal the animosity that the abolition movement and the Civil War had engendered. Today the trail drives live in song and story and on many a stirring canvas.

Baylis John Fletcher, the cowboy who later wrote of his adventures on the Chisholm Trail in 1879, was still a few months under twenty years old when he started off with the cattle outfit that spring. Born at Lexington, Texas, on July 4, 1859, he had grown up in livestock country in the trying Civil War and Reconstruction periods. Both his father and his mother were from pioneer families that had been following the frontier westward.

The father, George Moore Fletcher, was the son of a Methodist minister of the same name. The grandfather had married Patsy Battle in Virginia and had gone to Buncombe County, North Carolina, as a minister. Later he moved to Jackson, Mississippi. George was the only one of his children to come to Texas.

The mother of Baylis, who before her marriage had been Rebecca Roddy, died on the day of his birth. Since his father had six other small children to look after, the new baby was taken into the home of his maternal grandparents, Major Ephraim Roddy and Harriet Earle Roddy. There the youngster soon became the special charge of his maiden aunt, Ellen Roddy.

The Roddys were of Irish and English ancestry. Grandfather Ephraim had been born a year after his parents came to the American colonies from Cork, Ireland. He had married Harriet Earle, daughter of Colonel John Earle, a wealthy planter and Revolutionary soldier who had come to South Carolina from Virginia, where his ancestor, also named John Earle, had brought a group of colonists from England in 1652.

Major Ephraim Roddy, the grandfather of Baylis Fletcher, was an attorney who had won a commission in the War of 1812. In 1828 he took his wife and children to western Tennessee. Three years later his adventurous spirit led him to move on to the wilds of Texas and join the Austin colony. He practiced law in San Felipe, where he came to know Stephen F. Austin and other Texas leaders of that day.

While Baylis was still in his infancy, the Roddy family moved to the frontier village of Liberty Hill, in Williamson County, at the edge of the hill country, where thickets of live oak and cedar enlivened the landscape. There Baylis attended school, along with the children of neighbor families, most of them of Scotch-Irish and English stock. The community was closely knit, with settlers ready to help each other in case of a calamity of nature or an Indian raid. Most of the people had strong religious convictions. The Roddys were members of the Presbyterian church.

After his grandparents died, Baylis lived with his Aunt Ellen until he came of age. Among people devoted largely to raising cattle, it was natural that, while still in his teens, Baylis should learn the arts of riding, roping, and branding. Proficiency in those arts was the way most open to making a living, earning the respect of his fellows, and gaining admiring glances from the girls.

By the time he was nineteen years old, Baylis stood five feet ten and weighed about 150 pounds. With dark eyes, ruddy complexion, and reddish-brown hair, he was as handsome as the next fellow, and his delight in telling jokes and stories helped to make him popular. Thus it surprised no one that he was chosen as one of those to ride north with a herd of Longhorns owned by one of his neighbors, Captain Tom Snyder.

Thomas S. Snyder, who had just turned forty, belonged to one of the most prominent families in the cow country. "No family in the West has made a larger contribution to the range cattle industry," wrote Gene M. Gressley, director of the Western History Research Center at the University of Wyoming. "The Snyder herds became the foundation for many of the large cattle outfits in Colorado, Nebraska, Montana, and Wyoming."

Tom Snyder had been born in Yazoo County, Mississippi, March 1, 1839. The first of his family to come to Texas had been his mother's father, Dr. Thomas Hale, from Virginia. Dr. Hale went to Kentucky, thence to Mississippi, and finally to Texas in the early 1850's. He settled near the village of Round Rock, on Brushy Creek, in Williamson County, where he found the climate agreeable, and lived to the age of ninety-six.

Tom's father was Charles W. Snyder, a Pennsylvania German. He was a farmer who had lost his money in the wildcat banks of Mississippi. He died early in 1840, when Tom was only eleven months old. Soon afterward, Susan, the mother, moved with her daughter and her three sons to southwestern Arkansas and then to Barry County, in southwestern Missouri. From there she moved to Texas.

Already one of Tom's brothers, tall, black-haired Dudley Hiram Snyder, who was six years older than Tom, had gone to the Lone Star State on horseback in 1854 and had begun working for his grandfather Hale. In the spring of 1856 he went back to Missouri. In the fall of that year he and the middle brother, John W. Snyder, brought to Texas a two-horse wagon loaded with twenty-five bushels of apples, which they sold, mainly in Austin. With apples scarce in

Texas, the brothers obtained a dollar a dozen or ten dollars a bushel. After their load had brought them about $250 in gold, they rented a farm from S. M. Swenson in Palm Valley, where they kept batch.

A late freeze in the spring of 1857 killed their crops, but the brothers made out by working for others, renting another farm, and dealing in Spanish horses from San Antonio and more apples from Missouri. Tom came to Texas with Dudley in the fall of that year, with two loads of apples, which they sold between Dallas and Austin, clearing $500 in gold.

In the spring of 1858, while Dudley went to San Antonio to buy Spanish horses, John and Tom planted a crop on a farm rented from Shirley Tisdale. Later in that year the brothers ordered from Kentucky the county's first threshing machine and used it to thresh wheat in the neighborhood. The mother of the Snyder brothers moved to Texas in that year, and her father, Dr. Hale, gave her two hundred acres of land four miles west of Round Rock.

The Snyder brothers profited from their enterprises, especially their trading in horses and mules, and soon they were able to go into cattle raising. In August, 1861, soon after the Civil War broke out, the three Snyders enlisted. Dudley, made a second lieutenant, trailed Texas beeves to Tennessee for use by the Confederacy. After paying gold for the cattle and selling them for a good price, he made the mistake of investing his and his brother's profit in Negro slaves, who soon afterward were freed.

In the war Tom saw considerable action. After enlisting in San Antonio, he served first in Company C of the Seventh Texas Cavalry, General H. H. Sibley's brigade, with his brother John as captain. In New Mexico, when Mexicans surrounded a party of thirteen soldiers, of whom he was one, Tom was fortunate in escaping unhurt. On the first day of 1863 he was one of 150 volunteers taking part in the Confederate recapture of Galveston. Later he was sent twice to Louisiana with Texas cattle, and he became purchasing agent for the Trans-Mississippi Army of the Confederacy.

The war left the Snyder brothers broke, but Dudley borrowed two hundred dollars in Houston. In the fall of 1865 the three bought two hundred work oxen at fifteen dollars a head and began hauling cotton from eastern Texas to Brownsville and Matamoros, where it brought a high price. Soon they had enough profit to get back into the cattle business. On February 20, 1867, Tom married Miss Lenora A. Bryson, by whom eventually he had nine children.

In 1868, after the Snyders bought 1,000 big range steers, from five to ten years old, John and Tom walked them up the new Chisholm Trail to Abilene, Kansas. On the way north, they lost about 150 steers to Osage Indians, but later they were compensated $2,500 from the government. On this first drive they cleared a little more than $4,000. In that year and the next, the Snyders also trailed Longhorn herds by way of the Horsehead Crossing of the Pecos River to Fort Union, New Mexico.

In 1870, Dudley and John Snyder became formal partners, with Tom operating independently but working closely with them. In that year the partners trailed two herds to Schuyler, Nebraska. Tom, who could not get away that season, sent up a herd, which they sold for him. The next year, Dudley and John took up four herds of about 1,000 head each. The partners sold one herd at Grand Island, Nebraska, on the North Platte River, and one at Cheyenne, Wyoming. Then they put their other two herds together, making 2,000 head, and contracted to deliver them to a buyer in Salt Lake City. Caught in a snowstorm on the Green River, with the horses exhausted, they regathered the herd and put it back on the trail after John Snyder sent forty fresh horses by train from Salt Lake.

In 1872, Tom took up two herds of about 1,000 head each. In a storm the two herds ran together, making a combined herd of 2,120 head, one of the largest on the trail that year. In Cheyenne, Tom sold his cattle to Montana ranchmen.

In the summer of 1872, the three Snyders bought about 5,000 head of mixed cattle in Ellsworth, Kansas, and in Cheyenne. Tom took them, in two herds, across the Rockies at South Pass and on to a winter range below the Bannock Indian Reservation, between Rock Creek and the Snake River, leaving enough hands to look after them. Later the cattle were sold, some of them to a Salt Lake firm for range delivery on Goose Creek in Nevada and others to the government for use on Indian reservations.

The Snyder trail drives continued. The biggest operation by Dudley came in 1877 when, in partnership with J. W. Iliff of Denver, he delivered 28,000 head of cattle in Colorado. His final drive was in 1885. The last of Tom's drives, however, was the 1879 one which is the subject of Baylis Fletcher's narrative. In that year Tom did not go up with the herd but went north by train to meet and sell the cattle, as often was done by owners after railroads were available.

Tom Snyder, prospering from his trail drives, moved his family into a big two-story house set in a lawn of well-cared-for grass and flowers. The house was furnished with thick carpets, full-length mirrors, and imported hand-carved furniture. Later he homesteaded a ranch of 23,040 acres in Mitchell County. When he sold that ranch, he retained 128,000 acres in Lamb County and bought 45,000 acres in Hockley County.

Still later Tom Snyder became a sheep rancher in New Mexico. With profits from wool and lambs, he organized the State Bank of Clayton, where he lived for five years. Like his brothers, he attained considerable wealth and was a strong supporter of Southwestern University at Georgetown, Texas. In 1925, Tom retired and moved back to Texas to live with one of his daughters, Mrs. Susie Snyder Pace of Dallas. He died there on February 28, 1934, on the eve of what would have been his ninety-fifth birthday.

Unlike the owner of the herd he had helped to trail north in 1879, Baylis John Fletcher soon afterward turned from cattle to other occupations. When his Aunt Ellen Roddy went to Hamilton County to spend her declining years with the family of her brother Joseph, Baylis returned to his father's home in Lexington. There he obtained a job in the general merchandise store of Nicholas Hester, who had come over from Germany in 1856. Baylis became interested in one of his employer's nine daughters, Marie Hester. He and Marie were married in 1885.

Turning from storekeeping to education, Fletcher obtained a teacher's certificate and became principal of the Lexington public school. In 1896 he was elected to the Twenty-fourth Texas Legislature. Following his two-year term as a lawmaker, Fletcher returned to Lexington and became a cotton buyer. He had learned this business while buying cotton for the Hester store.

In 1900, after the Lee County treasurer, Israel Duey, died suddenly, Fletcher was appointed to fill out his term. On May 1 of that year, he moved with his wife and four children to the county seat, Giddings, where, a few weeks later, a fifth child was born. In Giddings he bought a large Georgian house facing the courthouse square. Built by a German immigrant in 1879, it had been used later to house a small Lutheran college.

Through repeated elections, Fletcher continued as county treasurer until 1911. During this period, he added to his income and helped support his family by buying cotton from the local merchants for a Houston firm. One of his avocations was attending the annual Confederate reunions held in various cities in the South. Cherishing a childhood memory of his Uncle Joe Roddy's leaving to join the Confederate Army, he escorted Lee County groups to reunions in distant cities.

Fletcher, who had joined the Methodist church in Lexington, since that town had no Presbyterian church, continued as a Methodist in Giddings, where for years he was superintendent of the Sunday school.

In Giddings, Fletcher also continued an avocation he had become interested in while still living in Lexington—writing historical articles related to his own experiences or those of members of his family. In 1900 he contributed to the *Texas Christian Advocate* an account of a religious camp meeting on Jenks Branch, where, as a barefoot boy, he had waded with others while waiting for the horn to be blown for starting the services. His next published piece was on the Big Springs train robbery in Nebraska in 1877, the site of which he had seen two years after the holdup. This article appeared in a Sunday issue of the *Denver Post,* April 18, 1909. One of his most interesting articles, which described chasing Indians after a raid when he was ten years old, appeared in the *Texas Magazine* for November,

1910. He also left in manuscript a piece, "The Regulators," dealing with his Uncle Joe Roddy's thwarting of an attempted lynching.

Baylis Fletcher's longest narrative, which remained unpublished until *The Cattleman* ran it serially in 1966, was "Up the Trail in '79," the account of his trip from Victoria, Texas, up the Chisholm Trail to Kansas and on to Wyoming.

Soon after he completed this chronicle, his health began to fail. In 1912, after a physical examination, he learned that he had an incurable disease, progressive muscular atrophy. He died on December 19 of that year, at the age of fifty-three. His widow lived on in the Giddings home until her final illness in 1956, in her ninety-fourth year.

Fletcher's trail narrative, although it was written years after the events it describes and thus lacks the immediacy of a day-by-day diary, nevertheless has a freshness that bespeaks close observation, a sharp memory, and better than ordinary ability in expression. It is among the longer and more detailed descriptions of trail drives, excluding the fictional ones, and it may take a high place as a revelation of what really happened when a Texas cow outfit went north with a herd of bawling Longhorns.

Contents

Illustrations

Up the Trail in '79

I

Gathering the Herd

———————◆————————

THE OPENING of a pioneer section of our country has always been accompanied by a certain amount of romance and adventure in connection with the removal of the settlers and their belongings to the virgin territory. New and unusually difficult routes have been opened, presenting problems and experiences to those traversing them. The nineteenth century saw a number of these trails blazed through the wilderness. The grim followers of Brigham Young moved their wagons and crude carts over the fateful Mormon Trail. The adventurous Forty-niners rushed to California over the tortuous Santa Fe Trail, the Overland Trail, and other routes. During the same period, the covered wagons of hardy settlers of the great Northwest were rumbling over the winding and dangerous Oregon Trail.

Scarcely less difficult were some of the passages leading to some of the less remote sections of the country. While the latter avoided the perilous mountain passes and desert regions, they traversed sections which still harbored the uncivilized red man and an assortment of wild animals and which suffered periodically from the seeming vengeance of the elements as they were visited by drouths, floods, and blizzards.

Such a route was the Chisholm Trail, which for nearly two decades following the Civil War led from Texas north to Kansas. This famous cattle trail afforded a wealth of material for adventure stories and legends.

[The Chisholm Trail was opened in 1867 by a young Illinois livestock dealer, Joseph G. McCoy. Located west of the earlier Shawnee Trail, it served an urgent need of Texas drovers, since the westward push of farm settlement had engulfed the old trail. Farmers resented the Longhorn herds, because, although themselves immune, they infected farm cattle along the route with a serious tick fever, then generally known as Texas fever.]

In the natural flow of emigration to the Western states and territories following the Civil War, vast ranges for grazing cattle were opened for ranch enterprises on the Western plains. These lands had been grazing grounds for millions of buffaloes. But the ceaseless warfare waged by hunters and adventurers against the noble bison had almost exterminated the wild cow of the Indian. Enterprising cattlemen saw profit in growing beef on the old buffalo ranges. But to stock such a large area with domestic cattle was a Herculean task.

Texas was the one great cattle country that could supply the demand for range cattle. Millions of cheap cattle were grazing on her boundless plains. Cattle prices were low in the Lone Star State, whereas in Colorado, Wyoming, Montana, and Dakota Territory, they were 100 per cent higher. Wire fences were almost unknown, and from the Red River to the Gulf of Mexico, with the exception of scattered settlements, Texas was one solid cattle range. [Barbed wire, which some cowmen regarded as an instrument of the devil,

4

was introduced into Texas in 1875. In 1879 it was being used in large quantity, but most of the ranges remained unfenced.] The drover who moved cattle from Texas to the plains of Wyoming had a profit of from five to ten dollars per head. The opening of the Western ranges was the opportunity for the Texas cattleman.

But Texas was far removed from the new territory. Railroads were few, and freight rates had not yet felt the effects of competition. The only practical means of transportation was to force the cattle to walk over the intervening space. This method led to the establishment of trails by which vast herds could be taken to the Northern ranges. The chief of these routes was the Chisholm Trail, called after a half-blood Scot-Cherokee who had traded in the region around the Arkansas River in the Indian Territory and southern Kansas.

The northern extremity of the Chisholm Trail, which was first at Abilene, Kansas, varied with the progress of railroad construction as the tracks of steel stretched westward through the region to the north. The cost of transportation by the trails was subject to business methods, and under careful management did not exceed two and a half dollars a head in large herds. Partnerships were formed by cattlemen who pooled their interests, and it was not uncommon for one firm to transport from 25,000 to 30,000 cattle in a single season. Each herd required a complete outfit of cowboys, a foreman or boss, a string of saddle horses, a horse herder, and a cook. The cook was also the driver of the grub wagon. A trail outfit usually included twelve or more men.

It was not surprising that many young men of the day sought jobs with the outfits going north. Some of the lads were interested primarily in the small financial gain, while others were imbued with the desire for adventure. I was still a youth of nineteen, but above fryin' size, when I took the trail fever. Doubtless I was prompted by the same spirit of adventure that had led my grandparents, by whom I was reared as an orphan, to leave their native South Carolina for the miasmic wilds of Tennessee, go down the Mississippi on a flatboat to New Orleans, and there take passage for Texas and Austin's colony on a vessel which was shipwrecked on the Texas coast near old Quintana during a tropical hurricane in 1831.

After the death of my grandfather, Major Ephraim Roddy, who as an attorney had settled first at San Felipe de Austin and moved to Washington-on-the-Brazos after the Revolution, and that of my grandmother, Harriet Earle Roddy, a most worthy member of a well-known South Carolina family, I became restless and expressed a desire to make a trip up the trail as a cowpuncher. My maiden aunt Ellen, who then had me in charge, remonstrated vigorously against the idea of a mere boy's going up the trail. She recounted tales of Indian attacks, stampedes, swollen streams, salty river crossings, and other adversities which confronted the trail driver. The Texas lad of pioneer days was an independent soul, however, and I finally met all of Aunt Ellen's objections. In the spring of 1879, I obtained a job with Thomas Snyder, a cattleman who lived in our home town of Liberty Hill, to help take a herd of South Texas cattle up the trail.

[Thomas Snyder, with his older brothers, Dudley Hiram Snyder and John W. Snyder, were members of a pioneer family who had come from Mississippi by way of Missouri, settled in Williamson County, and become prominent Texas cattlemen.]

6

Baylis John Fletcher, aged about thirty-seven

Thomas S. Snyder, owner of the herd

In company with other young men from Williamson and Burnet counties, I was to gather cattle bought by Mr. Snyder from John Green, who owned a ranch in Victoria County, on Coleto Creek, just south of Victoria. He had bought a whole "mark and brand," which meant all the cattle of a certain mark and brand, upon an estimate of their number. Such trades were not uncommon in Texas at that time. Tom Snyder simply gave John Green ten thousand dollars for all the cattle he had in the V Fleur-de-lis L brand.

Our party left Liberty Hill on March 10, 1879, for the Victoria ranch. The outfit consisted of George Arnett, who was to be our boss, eight cowboys, a cook, and a wagon and team. We started with a few saddle horses but depended on buying most of our cow ponies in South Texas. After stopping at several farms to buy a few horses, we arrived at sunset at the village of Round Rock, north of Austin. We spent our first night camped on the bank of Brushy Creek, where the noted train robber, Sam Bass, had been mortally wounded the preceding July. Early on the following morning we were ordered to allot the horses on hand. We determined by drawing who should have the first choice, and so on to the last. In this manner we drew our mounts until the supply was exhausted. The complete allotment for each man was eight horses. On the second day we crossed the Colorado River at Austin and camped near the Deaf and Dumb Institute, as it was then called.

On the third day, as we were riding along the Austin and Lockhart road in Onion Creek Valley, a little incident occurred which illustrated the piety of Tom Snyder. We were joined by a youth from that vicinity, one who apparently had formed his idea of cowboys from dime novels. He aired his lungs by cussing everything from his cow pony to the minister we met in the road. His language was sulphuric, with a rich assortment of oaths. He seemed astonished that we did not try to compete with him.

At last Mr. Snyder, who no longer could endure such a flow of profanity, turned to the youth and said, "Young man, we will be pleased to have your company if you will not swear so much, but if you can't quit cussing, please fall behind or ride ahead of us. We propose to be gentlemen."

Astonished, the boy rode in silence for several minutes. Then, giving Mr. Snyder a furtive glance, he asked, "Mister, is you a Christian?"

"I hope so," was the reply.

"And a cow driver?"

"Yes, why not?" said Mr. Snyder.

"That's awful damn strange," shouted the boy as he put both spurs to his horse and galloped away as if the heel flies were after him.

From Lockhart we passed through a timbered country with some gravelly roads. While we were in this belt of oaks, Sam Allen, one of our men, rode up to a farmhouse and inquired the price of eggs.

"Five cents," was the farmer's reply.

"Six dozen for two bits?" coaxed the avaricious cowpuncher.

"Yes," said the farmer.

That night we had the entire lot of seventy-two eggs scrambled for supper.

We crossed the Southern Pacific Railroad at Harwood and soon emerged from the timber at Peach Creek, coming out upon a beautiful rolling prairie at the German village of Hochheim. A day later we passed through the little town of Cuero, then the terminus of the Morgan Railway, built out from the port of Indianola. On the next morning we arrived at Victoria, where we forded the Guadalupe River to reach Green's Ranch. Coleto Creek, on which the ranch was situated, is famous as the stream near which Colonel James W. Fannin and his men were captured by the Mexicans a few days after the fall of the Alamo, only to be butchered a few days later near Goliad.

Before going out on the first roundup of V Fleur-de-lis L cattle, Mr. Snyder discharged our cook, who was a worthless scamp and a belly cheater, and for awhile we were compelled to follow the culinary art by turns. Then he hired two good Mexicans, one as a cook and the other as a remuda man or horse herder. Then he bought forty additional saddle horses from some Mexicans at fifteen dollars each. Our supply of horses thus was augmented to eighty animals.

The winter had been dry, and we soon learned that the cattle were poor and dying of starvation. We were told, however, that few were really dying natural deaths but that a band of cattle thieves, taking advantage of this condition, were killing and skinning the cattle. At night, it was said, they would round up some lean cows and drive them into the bogs, where they would die. Then they would drag them out for their skins. In those days of careless plenty on the ranches, whoever found a dead cow might skin her with impunity. Armed men were patrolling the ranges to protect the cattle against these thieves. Several fights had taken place with the bandits, and some of them had been slain.

Mr. Snyder hired a guide to pilot us through the range, and, since he was familiar with the brands, we were assured that he would help us find all the V Fleur-de-lis L cattle. Accordingly, Jim Andrews, our guide, soon organized a

grand roundup. As the youngest of the cowboys, I was detailed to remain at camp so that I could go daily into Victoria and get the mail and do the shopping.

Three outfits joined on the first grand roundup, each
representing a different brand. The range was unfenced,
and everybody's cattle were mixed promiscuously. The custom was for all the horsemen to go out on the prairie and,
with the eye, survey a limited area, say three miles in diameter, and then run everything together in one common herd.
Then part of the men were detailed to hold the horses while
others, called cutters, were sent into the common herd to
cut, or run out, such cattle as they severally claimed, putting the cuts of each brand into separate herds held by
men detailed for that purpose. When the cutters were
through, they had three small herds of cuts for the three
outfits. The remaining cattle were turned loose, and the
operation was repeated at another point on the range.

One evening as I returned from Victoria, I saw a vast
herd of cattle near our camp at the Green Ranch. Approaching, I was told that our outfit and two others had rounded
up the prairie north of the ranch and had assembled eight
or ten thousand cattle, too late in the afternoon to cut out
that night, and that they would be held until the following
morning. I was told to repair to camp at once and, after
changing horses, to report for night duty.

To eat supper, change horses, and return to the herd was
the work of a few moments. To hold all this vast drove of
untrained cattle intact seemed hardly possible, however, for
in the herd were many cows possessing young calves from
which they had been separated, and their motherly instincts
were asserting themselves in efforts to elude the vigilance
of the herders. I was to stand guard until midnight and then
be relieved by another man. But when the shades of night

10

excluded the rays of sunlight, a long line of ominous thunderheads appeared above the northern horizon.

"We're going to have a wet norther," muttered a seasoned veteran of the cow trail as we passed our round.

Vivid flashes of lightning, at intervals at first but rapidly growing in frequency as the night advanced, illumined the black crescent that now extended from the extreme northeast to the northwest. Soon the mutterings of distant thunder were distinctly audible. Then a dark roll of cloud rushed across the sky from the north, obscuring every star. A cold north wind brought a blinding rain, mingled with hail, and swept furiously across the prairie. The darkness soon became so dense that objects were scarcely discernible, even under the lightning's flashes. I soon found myself encircled by the bellowing herd.

"Will they stampede?" I called to a comrade revealed by a flash of lightning.

"No, not as long as the lightning flashes," said the puncher. "Get on the outside of the herd. They are drifting badly."

Pushing my way southward, I soon reached the front of the moving herd, where I found the entire force of the three outfits trying to check the advance of the excited cattle. The crest of the storm soon passed over, and the lightning flashes and the roar of thunder died away in the distant south. The cold rain driven by the chilling blasts of old Boreas continued. The darkness was complete. The drifting herd, however, was checked at last, several miles from the spot where the norther first struck us. Frequent collisions now occurred between cowboys riding in opposite directions; but they rode slowly, and such accidents provoked only merriment.

Our well-oiled pommel slickers had kept us dry, and all

hands remained in the saddle until dawn, when we of the first shift were told that we were relieved for the night. Appreciating the grim humor of this announcement, we rode away to camp, washed our breakfast down with black coffee, and sought the horse herd for fresh mounts. I was told to rope the best horse I had for a day's work and to return to the herd for cutting out our cattle. Happy Jack, my best horse, was not in a happy mood on that cold, wet morning; and as soon as he felt my weight in the saddle, he began to buck as if he had a bellyful of bedsprings. I was accustomed to riding broncos, but Happy Jack did some new stunts, and soon I found my center of gravity far removed from the base on which I tried to sit.

Fortunately, the tail of my slicker hung for a moment on the horn of my saddle, braking the force of my descent, and the softness of the wet ground mitigated my pain when I landed head-foremost amid the deafening applause of the cowpunchers. As soon as I was able to sit up, I saw Happy Jack in the dim distance, still bucking in frantic efforts to rid himself of the saddle also. A comrade soon roped the renegade and led him back to camp. Encouraged by cheers and goaded by criticism, I mounted Happy Jack again and rode away in triumph to join in cutting the V Fleur-de-lis L's from the big herd.

Hundreds of cattle had escaped during the stormy night, but we cut out 321 head of the proper brand from that big roundup. Albert Cochran and I were placed in charge of this small herd, with orders to graze them along Coleto Creek during the day and to corral them at the ranch that night. The combined outfits were to make another big roundup in Mission Valley, an early site of the old Spanish mission, La Bahia, which was removed to Goliad. [The mission and presidio of La Bahia, established in 1722 near

Matagorda Bay, had been moved in 1726 to a point on the Guadalupe River seven miles southeast of the present Victoria. In 1749 they were moved from that site, later known as Mission Valley, to the San Antonio River near the present town of Goliad.]

Our task at herding was easy, and the next three days passed pleasantly. Then Mr. Snyder rented a pasture for the cattle, relieving us of herd duty. The Mission Valley roundup had added 350 to 400 cattle to our collection.

I was now ordered to select three good horses from my allotment and join the next roundup. We crossed Coleto Creek and rode away to the west until we came to Captain Fleming's ranch on the San Antonio River. There we established a camp and prepared for a grand roundup on the following day. Early after sunrise we were in the saddle and extended our line of cowpunchers to a circle about two miles in diameter and began to drive everything toward a common center. Those range cattle had been worked so often that they knew their duty as well as we did, and we had little trouble as we contracted our circle of horsemen.

Soon each outfit began cutting its cattle out for separate bunches. Out of this roundup we got about two hundred of the cattle we were hunting. Taking those along, we followed the valley of the San Antonio River to a point where only a narrow strip of prairie separated the timber of the Guadalupe River bottom from that of the San Antonio. There, on the following day, we rounded up the range and found about 250 additional Snyder cattle. We now drove our herd thus augmented to the pasture near Green's Ranch.

Big roundups did not pay now, as the range was so depleted of the particular brand we sought and what remained were so scattered that it was advisable to divide our forces into small squads of four men each and to substitute pack horses for the grub wagon which had followed the big roundup. A guide familiar with the country was sent with each detachment. The river bottoms were dense, and in some places it was necessary to use trained dogs to run the cattle out of the thickets. Some of the wild ones would fight furiously when surrounded by horsemen or held at bay by the dogs. The wildest we roped and hogged down by tying their feet together with small cords of rope until the herd could be brought to them.

Once surrounded by other cattle, they were released with impunity, as the wildest steer will not fight in a drove of other animals. On one occasion Sam Allen was hogging down a big wild steer he had roped and thrown to the ground by dextrously riding around the beast and entangling its feet with his rope. His trained cow horse was holding the rope tight by the horn of the saddle as Sam tied the feet. Then suddenly the steer regained his feet and rushed at the puncher to gore him with his horns. Sam easily ran beyond the reach of the rope attached to his saddle horn. The steer rushed at the horse, but before the horse could be gored, a companion of Sam spurred to the scene and roped the steer, again throwing him to the ground. This time he was securely tied and the herd was brought up for his release.

Such performances were attended now and then with great danger. These acts were repeated from day to day until we had about all the Snyder cattle in the pasture.

About the sixth of April it was announced that the range work was completed and that a local man would gather and sell for the account of Mr. Snyder all the straggling cattle in his brand. We had collected about two thousand cattle and were ready to hit the trail. Before starting on our long journey, however, we must road-brand our cattle.

14

Our road brand was TL connected. To burn those letters on the sides of two thousand cattle, we must first drive them into the customary chute, or narrow lane, just wide enough for one cow to squeeze through and long enough to hold about twenty-five animals. After we had branded the imprisoned cattle by poking the red-hot branding iron through the fence of the chute, we cropped their tails as an additional mark to indicate that they were trail cattle. [Tom Snyder registered the TL connected brand in the Mark and Brand Book in the office of the county clerk of Victoria County on April 7.]

The branding required two days of hard work. Then, after other preliminaries had been arranged, on April 10, 1879, we were ready to start north. Before our departure on the long drive, several of our boys obtained a leave of absence for a day to run down to the port of Indianola and bathe in the Gulf. And on the night before we started, we had a grand stag dance at our camp on the Green Ranch. Mexican guitar pickers furnished the music, while festive cowboys danced waltzes in the warm embrace of another wearing spurs, leather leggings, and broad-brimmed sombreros. The hilarity lasted until after midnight, then we turned in for a last sleep on the ranch.

II

Pointing to the North

ON THE MORNING of April 11, a supreme moment for us, we started up the trail to Cheyenne, Wyoming. To gather the cattle in the pasture into one great herd took up the forenoon. In the afternoon we made only about five miles, bedding our cattle that night just south of Victoria, near the Guadalupe River. On the following morning we forded the river, which was low.

When we were passing through the streets of Victoria, a lady, fearful that the cattle would break down her fence and ruin her roses, ran out to the pickets and, waving her bonnet frantically at the cattle, stampeded those in front. With a dull roar, they charged back upon the rear of the herd, and but for the discreet management of boss Arnett, heavy damage to city property would have resulted.

"Give way at all street crossings and let the cattle have room," he shouted as he galloped about, giving orders to save the City of Roses from a disaster.

We complied quickly and soon had half a dozen residence blocks surrounded by excited and infuriated cattle. Soon they became so confused that the stampede was ended. We gave their fears time to subside, then drove them quietly out of the city without doing any serious damage.

On the second night, when we were camped near the source of Spring Creek, a real midnight stampede occurred. All hands were called to the saddle, and it was near dawn before we could return to our pallets for rest. We proceeded to the north and, in a few days, reached the mouth of Peach Creek, north of Cuero, where we paid for the privilege of watering in the big Kokernot pasture. [This presumably was a part of the Kokernot Ranch established by David L. Kokernot in 1855. Born in Holland in 1805, Kokernot came to New Orleans in 1817 and to Texas in 1832. He served in the Texas Revolution and with Terry's Texas Rangers in the Civil War. He died in 1892.]

Here water was procured in the Guadalupe River, and we stopped on its banks to rest our cattle and eat dinner. While grazing the cattle along the bank of the river, we discovered a big alligator idly floating on the water's surface. All hands were attracted by the strange sight and began shouting at the big saurian, who protected himself by sinking out of sight in the turbid waters.

After dinner Joe Felder took off his boots and washed his feet in the river. Then he sat on the root of a big tree facing the stream and fell asleep. Manuel García, our cook, with that levity characteristic of the Mexican, conceived a practical joke. Throwing a log so that it fell into the river just in front of the sleeping Joe, he shouted, "Alligator!" In a quick effort to rise, Joe slipped into the river, going entirely under and rising by the side of the floating log, which he mistook for the alligator. He screamed for help, and stake ropes were thrown him, which he seized frantically, to be drawn out, as he thought, from the jaws of death. His disgust was profound when he discovered that he was escaping only from a rotten log.

On the following night we bedded our cattle in a short, wide lane between high rail fences a few miles east of Gonzales. This was a thickly settled region, timbered with a variety of oaks, and the surface was covered with gravel. My shift at guard duty was the last in the night, and at about two A. M., Sam Allen, Carteman García, and I were called to go on herd. Allen and I were stationed at the east end of the lane, while the Mexican guarded the other end. The night was frosty, and as the cattle seemed to be sleeping soundly, Sam and I dismounted and built a fire of dry branches by which to warm. At first we would warm by turns and ride time about. But everything was so still that we became careless and both dismounted at the fire, where we began to spin yarns. As the bright fire lit up the scene, it was beautiful to behold. Two thousand cattle rested quietly, lying down and chewing their cuds.

Suddenly there was a loud and ominous roar, while a cloud of dust obscured our vision.

"Stampede!" shouted Sam as he let loose his bridle reins and sprang behind an oak, which he hugged with both hands. I did not have time to turn Happy Jack loose but threw my arms around Allen on the side of the tree opposite the herd. We were none too quick, for now the horns of the stampeding bovines were raking the bark from the opposite side of the oak as they rushed madly past us. It was a moment of supreme terror, but only a moment. In less time than it takes to relate it, the cattle had passed us and, mounting Happy Jack, I was in full pursuit.

I soon overtook the cattle, pressed on past them, and

turned their leaders back. They now formed a circle, where they milled in one great wheel, revolving with almost lightning velocity. By holding them in this mill, I soon had them confused, and they began to bellow to one another. I had learned that these were welcome sounds in a stampede. As soon as the bellowing becomes general, the run begins to subside. Of course, such a revolving wheel cannot be stopped suddenly. The momentum they have acquired makes it necessary to slow down the cattle gradually, or else the ones that stopped first would be trampled to death.

I now heard a voice shouting, "Stay with them, Fletcher." In a moment I was joined by Mr. Snyder, riding one of the wagon horses bareback and with a blind bridle. "Where is Sam?" he asked. But I did not know.

We soon had the cattle quiet, and as it now was about dawn, we drove them back to the bed ground. I learned from Mr. Snyder that something had frightened the cattle in about the middle of the lane where we had bedded them and that I was holding only a part of the herd, the remainder having run out of the other end of the lane past García. Thinking that the whole herd had gone that way, the cowboys had all gone to the aid of García, but when Allen and I were missed, Mr. Snyder had gone in search of us. When Allen's horse was found loose with the saddle on, it was supposed that the horse had fallen with him as he rode out ahead of the cattle and that he had narrowly escaped being trampled to death.

We did not confess until long afterward that we had been caught off our horses by the stampede and that Allen had let his horse go. Such admissions were not expected on the trail. After getting the fragments of our herd together, we strung them out in a thin line, and as they passed a certain point, the cattle were counted. It was found that we were about one hundred head short. That many evidently had escaped in the stampede.

While we were discussing the feasibility of recovering the lost cattle, four hard-looking citizens rode up and said, "Had a stampede last night, did you?" We answered in the affirmative. Then the strangers offered their services to help put the cattle back in the herd. Their offer was to bring in all they could find for one dollar per head. Mr. Snyder then offered them fifty cents per head, to which they readily agreed. It seemed plain to us that these accommodating gentry had stampeded our herd for this revenue.

They were joined by recruits, and during the day they delivered sixty cattle bearing our road brand. We still were forty short, but time was precious. Mr. Snyder said that the missing ones would go back to the range near Victoria and be gathered there for his account and that we must proceed. Later our own scouts brought in about twenty additional renegades, so that we were only about twenty short when we started forward on the following day.

Moving a large herd through a timbered country was attended with many difficulties. Sometimes a stubborn brute would take to a thicket and fight with wild fury any puncher who tried to dislodge him. In a rocky thicket near Plum Creek one old cow took refuge, and when Poinsett Barton entered on foot to drive her out, she made a desperate lunge to gore him. Barton hurled a stone, striking her in the forehead. Her skull was crushed, and she fell dead. Barton was brought before the boss for killing a cow, but he pleaded self-defense and was acquitted, with a warning not to place himself again in such a position as to make the death of a cow necessary to protect his life.

Suitable bed grounds were difficult to find on this part

of the trail. We made use of a line of picket corrals which enterprising residents had erected, and regular herders were stationed around the big pen to watch that the cattle did not escape. For awhile all was quiet, but late in the night the herd stampeded and broke down the fence, giving us another night in the saddle for all hands.

In this stampede, which was on a Saturday night, I lost my hat. On the following morning we came to a country store just south of Lockhart. I called at the home of the merchant and asked him if he kept hats. He said he did. Then I told him of my predicament and asked him to sell me one. He replied that he was sorry for me but that under no circumstances would he sell a hat on the Sabbath. I implored him, speaking of "the ox in the ditch," but he was inexorable in his determination. So I had to ride all day bareheaded. On the next day we arrived at Lockhart, where I rode into town and bought a hat.

The weather in the spring of 1879 was extremely dry. The supply of water along the trail was so scant that often we had to fill our barrel for drinking water from tanks, as the dirty ponds made by the damming of ravines were called. Since this water was contaminated, we were attacked by sickness in the camp. I had fever several days but kept it secret from fear of being sent home.

Anderson Pickett, a Negro Mr. Snyder took along as his servant, came to me one night while I was on herd and said, "Look heah, boy, I know youse sick, ain't yer?"

"Yes," I said. "I'm sick tonight."

"Den you des' let me herd in yo' place. You des' lay down here under dis here mesquite tree, an' I wakes you up 'fo' day." I was too sick to refuse the proffered aid. Dismounting, I gave the reins of old Happy Jack to Anderson, who faithfully did my guard duty until dawn, waking me as promised in time to prevent detection. This relief was of great benefit to me.

We forded the Colorado River at old Webberville, a few miles below Austin. As we drove our cattle across the river, we heard the booming of a cannon in the direction of the capital city. It was April 21, and the people were celebrating the anniversary of the battle of San Jacinto, which had changed the course of Texas history just forty-three years earlier.

[On that day about a thousand Austin citizens, including several veterans of the battle of San Jacinto, gathered at the fairgrounds for the eleventh annual celebration and basket picnic of the Austin fire department. The entertainment included horse races, a baseball game, a military drill by the Austin Greys, and shooting at glass balls. Herzog's band played all day, and dancing continued through the day and into the evening.]

We camped near Manor, where I went to a physician and had a prescription filled. My fever, however, continued to rise every day, and my legs were so swollen that I had to split the uppers of my boots to get them on. My condition was such that I could no longer conceal it. And now it began to rain. All night long the rain poured in torrents. We had reached Brushy Creek north of Manor and near Hutto Station. The pain from inflammatory rheumatism in my ankles was excruciating. We forded Brushy at Rice's Crossing, and Mr. Snyder, learning of my condition, told the faithful Anderson to take me to some farmhouse where I could be cared for and kept dry.

The Negro did his best to comply, but every application for shelter was refused, until we became discouraged. I thought I should have to give up and die of exposure in the cold, blinding April rain. But Anderson persevered. "Yon-

22

A Drove of Texas Cattle Crossing a Stream

Cowboys at the Chuck Wagon

der is a little rent house," said he. "Mebbe-so we kin git you in dar." Sure enough, the poor renter had not the heart to drive me away. My host and hostess, who had recently married, received me kindly.

Anderson explained that I was one of Tom Snyder's cowboys and that I was sick. The big young fellow said, "Bring him in. We have only one room and are not fixed to entertain, but I have been on the trail myself, and I can't turn off a sick puncher in this rain." I was helped into the cabin as Anderson led my horse away.

Seeing how I was suffering, the tender-hearted young woman burst into tears. "Take our bed, and we will sit up for you," she said.

"No," said I, "just spread my blanket and slicker on the floor. That's all the bed I need."

That night, when all was still and I was supposed to be asleep, I overheard my case discussed by my hosts. "Oh, goodness, John! The boy can't live. Oh, it's awful to be sick on the trail. We could not turn him off to die in this rain. Do you think he will live?"

"You can't tell anything about it, Lucy," came the deep drawl of the husband. "I have been mighty sick on the trail, but I never died. We must do our duty and take care of him until he dies or gets better. That's all we can do."

The cabin had a fireplace, and my host kept a fire all night near my feet. The next morning I felt much improved, but my feet were so swollen that I could not put on my boots. A hot foot bath reduced the swelling, and in the afternoon I was able to sit up. Reaction was now so favorable that on the second morning, at my request, my host carried me on one of his horses to our camp. He refused to accept any pay for my entertainment.

The rainstorm had passed away, and the sun was shining when I rejoined our outfit. Mr. Snyder said I must go home on a sick discharge, as I would not be able to endure the hardships of the trail. I begged him not to dismiss me. He finally agreed to try me awhile longer but told Mr. Arnett to discharge me when we reached Fort Worth if I were not well. My health, however, gave me no more trouble.

Sam Allen, Andy Marcus, and John Ledbetter quit the outfit at Hutto, where new men were hired to take their places. Mr. Snyder also went back to his home at Liberty Hill, turning over the entire responsibility of the trip to our foreman, George Arnett. His faithful Negro, Anderson Pickett, also left us, finding work with a drove of saddle horses bound for Wyoming.

We forded the San Gabriel River near Jonah, a few miles east of Georgetown. Crossing Possum Creek, we followed the Belton road to a bridge on the Lampasas River. Fearing to risk the bridge, we made a detour of several miles and crossed the stream at Saul's Mill. Just as the leaders of our herd came opposite the mill, they took fright at the noise of the machinery and rushed back on the rear cattle. For half an hour the whole herd milled on the bank before we could force them to cross the stream.

Our next camp was on Salado Creek near the village of Salado. There, on the night of May 4, we were caught in a hailstorm that made our cattle drift badly. The severe hail lasted only a few moments, but our heads and shoulders were bruised by the falling ice, and it was many hours before we could quiet the excited cattle. We found the next day that a few miles north of us the hail was so severe that birds, rabbits, and domestic fowls were beaten to death and many crops destroyed. During the hail our saddle horses had stampeded, and we found on taking stock the next morning that two horses were missing. I was detailed to hunt for them and to follow the herd, which crossed the Leon River at Belton. I found only one of the runaways, and by hard riding I overtook the herd that night.

We now entered a more broken country among the hills of McLennan County. We passed to the west of Waco, entering Bosque County at Valley Mills. While camped on Steele's Creek in Bosque County, we had one of the biggest stampedes of the entire trip. That night a coyote was seen to enter the bed ground of the herd, frightening the cattle and causing them to run. The country was open, and the only loss we suffered was that of a much-needed night's rest. We halted here a day or two to look for a saddle horse that had escaped from Poinsett Barton with a long stake rope attached to it. It was the best horse allotted to him and never was recovered. Perhaps it became entangled by the stake rope in the thickets which covered the hills in that section and perished from starvation.

We were now having a great deal of trouble finding pasturage for our cattle. As long as we kept to the plain beaten trail, we were not molested. But the moment we turned aside to graze our cattle, the settlers came to us, claimed the land upon which our herd was grazing, and ordered us to get off the grass. Under the law, we had to comply quickly or sustain an action for damages. We often doubted the ownership claimed to the grazing lands, but as we had no time to investigate titles, the only safe thing we could do was to move on. We crossed the Brazos River at the old mountain village of Kimball and passed through Johnson County just west of Cleburne. We now had a delightful stretch of prairie, sparsely settled, until we neared Fort Worth. Grass was abundant, and we were rarely molested while seeking forage for our herd.

[In its issue of May 8, the *Fort Worth Democrat* listed

25

the Snyder herd of 2,525 head as having been reported in on the preceding day. Thus it passed Fort Worth ahead of the peak of the season's drive.]

Fort Worth, with a population of about ten thousand, was then the terminus of the Texas and Pacific Railway and was the last trading point where we could buy supplies on the trail until we should reach Dodge City, Kansas. We were given a day of rest, and, dividing the hands into two shifts, Mr. Arnett said he would allow each of us half a day in town. He planned to buy provisions to last two months. By the Chisholm Trail it was five hundred miles from Fort Worth to Dodge.

Solicitors from the big grocery stores of Fort Worth met us on horseback several miles from the city, bringing such gifts as bottles of whisky and boxes of fine cigars. Steve Pointer, known as Shug in our outfit, was the oldest cowpuncher we had, and looking older than Mr. Arnett, he often was mistaken for the boss. Frequently the mistake worked to Shug's advantage, though there would come a time when he regretted that he did not look more like a cowpuncher.

The drummers from Fort Worth all wanted to see the boss, who was purchasing agent for the outfit, and by previous arrangement Shug played his part well, accepting a box of fine cigars, some whisky, and other blandishments. Mr. Arnett quietly trailed the cattle while Shug stopped to talk with the drummers. After he thought Shug had accepted all that was due him, Will Bower rode swiftly to the rear and shouted to the erstwhile boss, "Shug, the boss says come on, you lazy cuss, and get to work, or he'll turn you off at Fort Worth." It then dawned upon the solicitors that they had been buncoed and that they would need a new supply of gifts to corral the real boss when he was

identified. Shug became angry at Will for interrupting his
game and made some uncomplimentary remarks.

Leaving Fort Worth, we followed the trail north, passing
in sight of Decatur to our left and Saint Jo to our right,
crossing parts of Wise, Denton, Cook, and Montague counties. Since Montague was a border county, we were told that
we could wear side arms without fear of arrest, so every
cowpuncher who had a six-shooter buckled it on just to
enjoy the privilege of carrying a weapon.

As we passed a farmhouse near Saint Jo, a fine Shorthorn bull broke out of a pasture and joined our herd. We
cut him repeatedly, but he followed on about a mile to a
point where we bedded our cattle for the night. The next
morning the indignant owner came to us and demanded
we take his bull back to the pasture, threatening to prosecute
us if we did not. We advised him to take the animal back
with him, but he haughtily refused to do so and threatened
to have us arrested for carrying pistols in Montague County. We promised that we would carry the animal no farther
but did not agree to take him back. He rode away in a great
rage, continuing his threats. After he had gone we roped
the bull, threw him down, hogged his feet together with
strong cords, and left him lying on the ground as we moved
our herd down the valley of Farmer's Creek to Spanish
Fort, where we were to cross the Red River and enter the
Indian Territory.

[Although most of the Chisholm Trail outfit crossed at
Red River Station, some still used the old crossing at Spanish Fort. This had been an Indian trading post and, as early
as 1719, was a supply point for French trappers. In 1759,
Diego Ortiz Parrilla tried to take the stockaded village but
was repulsed. Later it came under Spanish control for a
time, and early Anglo-American settlers gave the site its
present name.]

27

On or about the first day of June we came in sight of the Red River Valley, beyond which we could see the Indian Territory. The country ahead was then a wilderness, without a human habitation in view of the Chisholm Trail to the line of Kansas, nearly three hundred miles away by the meanderings of our route.

As we were gazing upon this distant prospect, several well-mounted horsemen rode up, and their leader informed Mr. Arnett that he was a cattle inspector, whose duty it was to inspect carefully every herd crossing the northern boundary of Texas, cutting out any estrays that might be in the herd not bearing the road brand of the outfit. We were instructed to string the cattle out in a line, so that they might be passed one or two at a time between the inspector and one of his assistants, to be examined carefully as to their ownership.

Four or five little dogies, as poor little orphan yearlings were called, had escaped our vigilance in cutting out strays, and they were taken out of the herd by the inspector and turned over to his assistants. After the inspection was over, Mr. Arnett paid the inspector his per capita fee for examining the herd, which in our case amounted to about seventy-five dollars.

[To prevent the trailing out of stray or stolen cattle, the Texas legislature in 1870 had authorized the governor to appoint cattle inspectors for counties needing them. Since this post carried no salary, it often was held by the sheriff or some other county officer. In the disorganized Reconstruction era, some unscrupulous men posed as cattle inspectors to extort money from the drovers. In 1873 one inspector made so many demands for money that a local newspaper called the practice "a genteel system of blackmail." An honest and more effective inspection was set up after the 1877 formation of the Stock Raisers Association of Northwest Texas, now the Texas and Southwestern Cattle Raisers Association.]

Having undergone this inspection, our herd was given a clean bill of health, and we were permitted to take the cattle across the Red River, which at this point was low and easily forded. The prospect of entering an uninhabited wilderness was a source of great joy to the cowboys. Civilization and cattle trailing were not congenial, and we had been greatly annoyed in the settled districts of Texas. Depending entirely on free grass for forage for our cattle and horses, we had constantly come in collision with the farmers, who wanted the grass for their domestic animals.

We were not alone on the trail. The big drive northward was at its height, and that spring there were probably 500,000 cattle and horses moving up the one universal trail from South Texas. Often we had been driven by angry men, with ferocious dogs, from tract to tract of grazing land, but our movements were so deliberate that the cattle got enough to live upon. The Indian Territory was the cowpuncher's paradise. Now we would have no more lanes, no more obstructing fences, but one grand expanse of free grass. It was a delightful situation to contemplate.

Our Mexican cook was unfortunate in crossing the Red River. He stopped his wagon in the middle of the stream to fill his water barrel. While he was doing so, the wagon settled to the axles in the yielding quicksands. The oxen were unable to move. Manuel began to beat them with his whip, and the oxen turned quickly to one side, breaking the tongue out of the wagon and leaving it bogged in the river. We went to his rescue and, cutting a cottonwood pole, lashed it with ropes to the broken wagon tongue. But the team could not move it. Finally, after we borrowed two

29

additional yokes of oxen from a neighboring outfit, the six big steers hauled the wagon out of the river. A dried cowhide suspended under the wagon like a hammock and known as the caboose or possum-belly held kindling wood, stake pins for our horses, and other implements for use on the trail. All of the contents that would float were lost, drifting away upon the reddish waters of the river.

III

Indian Country

SINCE THERE WERE NO TREES where we camped on our first night in the Nation, as that country was called, we had to bury the knots at the ends of our stake ropes in the hard prairie soil instead of tying to stakes when we picketed out our night horses.

Being in a wilderness now, free from all the restraints and annoyances of civilization, we decided to rest for a day, graze our cattle, and celebrate by killing a fat yearling. Our facilities for curing fresh meat on the trail were so poor that we had subsisted principally on bacon, dried beans, and bread. Killing a beef on the trail was a great waste, as only a small part of the meat could be eaten before it spoiled. To minimize the waste, we chose a fat yearling, a stray that had eluded the vigilance of the inspector.

An abundant supply of the meat was broiled for supper, and the remainder was spread upon the flesh side of the hide on the ground near the wagon. When I was called to go on herd duty that night, I found two coyotes feasting on our beef. I refrained from shooting them on account of my sleeping comrades. I drove them away, but they hung around and stole enough to satisfy their hunger.

Leaving our first camp in the Indian Territory, we soon entered the belt of post-oak forest in the neighborhood of Mud Creek and Wild Horse Creek. The oaks were scattering, and their branches had been scorched by grass fires to such a height that the country was practically an open prairie. The grass was excellent, and, to recuperate our nearly famished cattle, we were ordered not to drive them on the trail but to keep them grazing toward the north. In this manner, with scarcely any effort, we moved them about six miles a day for three consecutive days. Our stock improved wonderfully under this plan.

Now that we were in the Nation, where there was no pistol law and nobody to enforce any law, our men continued to indulge in their penchant for toting six-shooters. All who had those weapons rubbed them bright and kept them belted on. I had brought no pistol, my only weapon being a Winchester carbine which hung in a leather scabbard from my saddle horn. We marched on now, armed to the teeth for savage foes and wild animals. At Fort Worth we had bought a good supply of ammunition, and we were prepared to stand a siege or head a revolution. With two exceptions, we were novices on the trail and little knew how useless our guns would be in these parts.

True, the country abounded in deer, antelopes, wild turkeys, and prairie chickens. There were also wolves, a few buffaloes and bears, and droves of wild horses or mustangs. To our disgust, however, we soon learned that all kinds of game fought shy of the Chisholm Trail, which was lined with herds, cattlemen with guns, wagons, and teams for hundreds of miles. We frequently saw deer, antelopes, and mustangs in the distance, but so wild were they that we rarely got within rifle shot of any of them. The carnage caused by our invasion was limited chiefly to the killing of

32

jack rabbits, prairie dogs, and rattlesnakes. After wasting much ammunition, we soon grew tired of such sport and returned our guns to the wagon.

One night while we were encamped on Wild Horse Creek, our saddle horses stampeded and ran several miles before we could check their flight. Carteman García, our remuda man shouted *"Los Indios!"* as he ran after the horses, indicating that they had been frightened by Indians. We were now only a short distance from the Comanche Reservation, and it was common for those redskins to steal away from the garrison and depredate on the trail. Their plan was to stampede droves of horses working on the trail, with the intent of stealing such animals as were lost in the stampede. As soon as we rounded up our horses and brought them back to the camp, they began to sniff the breeze and run again.

"There are Indians about here, and they are trying to steal some of our horses," said Arnett, as he detailed three men including myself to help the Mexican watch the horses until dawn. We went on picket duty heavily armed but saw no sign of any enemy. On the following day we could see the Wichita Mountains about the reservation at Fort Sill, not more than twenty-five miles away.

After crossing the Little Washita and Big Washita rivers, we left the cross timbers and came out on a beautiful expanse of fertile prairie lands. Here we found those little rodents known as prairie dogs. For these playful animals the word dog is, of course, a misnomer. There is nothing canine about them. A species of ground squirrel, of social habits, they live in cities of many thousand inhabitants called dog towns. As one approaches a dog town, the inhabitants of the town sit at the entrances to their burrows and utter a cry of alarm much resembling the bark of a small dog. This sound is called barking, and hence the name dog is applied to the squirrel that barks so much.

In a dog town it is said that the burrows frequently are inhabited by rattlesnakes. These underground homes are all connected by subways, so that the dog can pass from burrow to burrow without coming to the surface. There was a belief among cowboys that the rattlesnakes were intruders who despoiled the homes of the dogs and devoured their young. Evicting the grown members of the dog family, the snake appropriated the burrow as his own. I was unable to verify this theory. I saw the snakes in the abandoned burrows, but whether they took peaceable or forcible possession, I am not able to state. Studying the habits of live rattlesnakes was not a fascinating pastime to me.

Besides those burrows devoted to snakes, many of the abandoned were occupied by a prolific species of owl—the burrowing owl. I could not determine whether the owls were intruders or peaceful squatters. Taking them all together, the dogs, the owls, and the snakes, the ground was densely populated. Another rodent found frequently in this vicinity was the little stripped ground squirrel that abounded also on the Staked Plains of Texas.

Not far from the Washita River we came to an elevated ridge of prairie called Monument Ridge. Upon the crest of the ridge were several heaps of stones, evidently piled by human hands to commemorate the savage triumph of some tribe over its enemy. From the remotest periods of human history, stones have been used to record historical events. We had no means of learning how long since the events here recorded had transpired.

[This landmark, known also as Monument Hill or Monument Rocks, is about twenty-seven miles north of the Red River and just east of the present village of Addington. It offered a fine view of the surrounding country. Cowboys on its summit could spot cook wagons and strung-out herds for ten to fifteen miles in either direction. The almost flat top of the hill was strewn with slabs and boulders of reddish sandstone. Early drovers gathered some of these rocks into two piles as markers for the trail. The piles were about three hundred feet apart, and each was about ten feet across and twelve feet high. Cowboys who climbed the hill later used their knives or spurs to carve their initials or brands on the soft stone.]

A great change now appeared in the character of the forage which our animals found. While grass was still abundant, it no longer was the tall blue sedge grass of the cross timbers. The ground was now covered with the short, nutritious wire grass, called buffalo grass. Dry and parched in places, it seemed to retain its nutriment. Our cattle and horses thrived wonderfully upon it.

About June 15 we came in sight of a long line of straggling trees standing directly across our course, and they seemed to be burning at the ground as clouds of what we took for smoke rose from the surface beneath them. We were informed that we were approaching the South Canadian River and that the apparent smoke was sand in drifting clouds, agitated by the wind sweeping the dry river bed. During a rainy season the Canadian was a river of great dimensions but shallow and full of treacherous quicksands. At this time, however, it was a dry zone of drifting sands, except where a small stream flowed in a narrow channel. The banks were long lines of sand dunes piled about thickets of wild plum bushes. Between this natural levee and the hills beyond the river was a valley of the richest verdure, where we grazed our herd for several hours. We camped that night just north of the river.

On the following morning, as we were going leisurely along the trail, we discovered that a band of Indians was riding rapidly in a circle around us, as if to estimate our strength. They followed one another in single file. After examining them through his field glass, Mr. Arnett said he thought they were reservation Indians, and he did not anticipate any attack by them. The Indians now paused at a safe distance and, after gazing at us for a few moments, started directly toward us in Indian file, following an old buffalo trail. When they had approached to within a few hundred yards of our herd, they all halted except their leader, who rode up alone, making signs which we construed as friendly. When he came within speaking distance, he asked for our chief.

Our thoughts turned immediately to Shug Pointer. If he was fond of posing as foreman, now was his time. We directed the Indian to Shug. He approached Shug, addressing him as "Chief." Shug grew wild-eyed and escaped by dashing right through the herd. The Indian followed in close pursuit. Shug was about to draw his gun when we remonstrated and told him he must play boss again. In the end it was necessary, of course, to direct the Indian to Mr. Arnett. The warrior began his importunities by announcing that he was Spotted Wolf, a Navajo chief.

"Mebbe-so white chief give Injun some beef," he said. "Injun mighty hungry. Squaw mighty hungry. Papoose mighty hungry. Injun have no supper for three days."

Mr. Arnett promised him a beef and told us to cut out a certain steer for him. As soon as we ran the animal out of the herd, the big buck signaled for the rest of the party to advance. They came up and, in a mixture of broken English and Spanish, begged the loan of some pistols. Several were supplied, and then began a grand chase after the poor steer. They either were poor marksmen or wished to prolong the pursuit of the animal by bad shooting. Though they rode at full speed beside the running steer, more than a dozen shots were fired into his anatomy before one struck a vital spot. In the chase were several squaws armed with long lances with which they tried to pierce the sides of the wretched steer.

Now that their victim had fallen, the Indians all dismounted and returned the guns. Hunting knives were drawn, and the hide was no sooner peeled off the beef than they all began to eat the raw flesh, still quivering with the nervous twitchings of the dying steer. Salt, fire, and water were not required. As soon as the abdominal cavity was opened, the ravenous creatures began to eat the raw intestines. They stopped at nothing but the bones. Their numbers were constantly augmented by new recruits from the prairie, and soon nothing was left of the steer but the hide and the well-scraped bones of his skeleton. A pack of hungry wolves could not have cleaned the carcass more quickly.

Now a second Spotted Wolf appeared on the scene. Heading another party of warriors, he denounced the first chief as an impostor and begged for beef. His party was given another small beef, which was eaten ravenously. As more recruits came every minute, it began to appear that a whole tribe had descended upon us and that our entire herd would be devoured. We had at least a hundred bucks and squaws standing around whining for more beef.

To our great relief, several well-armed Indians suddenly rode up and announced that they were Indian police and were armed to hold the reservation Indians under control. They informed us that both the "chiefs" were impostors and that the real Spotted Wolf was sick at Fort Reno. They ordered the bucks back to the fort. But they were not heeded well by the begging savages; it was late at night before the last of the creatures left us, and not until they had begged for everything in the grub wagon.

My ideal of the Indian had been formed from reading James Fenimore Cooper's tales and other romantic narratives. I was speedily disillusioned when I met the real thing. The human being in a state of savage neglect is the most repulsive object known to civilized mankind. The odor emitted by the bodies of these poor wretches was horrible, and their habits will not admit of description here. When at last they all departed, the sympathy I had felt for the poor outraged red man was gone.

On the following morning we saw a man in a wagon driving, as we thought, aimlessly over the plain. He stopped here and there and seemed to be loading something into his wagon. Approaching him, we asked his business. He informed us that he was a bone man. This, we were told, meant a man whose occupation was to gather buffalo bones on the plains and haul them to market. He was hauling his load to Abilene, Kansas. Later we found that bone gathering was an occupation followed by many adventurers. The bones of buffaloes were abundant where no picker had been. I counted the scattered skeletons of nearly a hundred bison around one pond, where the animals had been shot as they were drinking. Most of the bones were still held together by ligaments. Some of the skulls showed where the deadly bullet of the big needle gun had penetrated the brain of the buffalo.

At other places we found as much as half a ton of broken bones in a heap. We were informed that these were places where Indian hunters had held great snake dances. The bones were broken to obtain the marrow, which was esteemed a great delicacy by both the Indians and the white hunters. It is not supposed that the Indians killed all the animals whose bones were thus broken; following in the wake of the destructive white hunters, they would gather the bones for a marrow feast. It mattered not if the marrow fat was putrid.

[Pioneer farmers quickly discovered that the buffalo skeletons that whitened the plains had a cash value. Gathering and selling bones enabled many a farm family to stay on their claim until they had a cash crop to sell. One man estimated that bones gathered on the Kansas prairies between 1868 and 1881 brought two and a half million dollars. In Texas and elsewhere bone-gathering was equally profitable. Most of the bones were converted into fertilizer, but some were used in refining sugar, and a few of the choice ones went into bone china.]

Moccasin tracks, as the peculiar footprints of Indians wearing moccasins were called, became common now. They were seen at the fords on all the streams. It was evident on every side that we were in the land of the red men. These signs kept us in apprehension of a raid upon our remuda by Indian horse thieves. Loss of saddle horses would be a calamity to any outfit going up the trail.

About this time Mr. Arnett met with a painful accident which disabled him for a time. He had roped a wild horse and, according to custom, had attached one end of the rope to the horn of his saddle. The bronco was running, and, before Mr. Arnett had a chance to turn his horse to check the momentum of the animal, it made a quick pull which threw his horse on its side, catching the rider's leg under its body. Arnett had been shot in that leg in the Civil War, and it was weak. The result was that he was so badly crippled that he was placed on a couch made for him in the wagon and had to rest there for about a week before he was able to ride again.

Mr. Arnett's crippled condition was a great misfortune to us. A body of men without a leader cannot succeed in any enterprise. But let a group of untrained cowboys, in a land where there is no legal restraint, try to conduct a herd of cattle with no recognized authority lodged in any one person, then they are like a ship's crew on a troubled sea without a captain. In our case, every man tried to exercise that authority which no one possessed, and personal difficulties of a serious nature were narrowly averted.

We had now reached the Cimarron River, which we crossed near the mouth of Kingfisher Creek. The water of this stream was low, barely flowing, and it was so salty that we scarcely could drink it. Soon after we had crossed to the other side, a horseman came to our camp and presented a letter from Mr. Snyder, authorizing him to pilot us through the region of the saline and gypsum waters. The rivers being low, the waters were so strongly impregnated with salts that many cattle had died from drinking them.

Our pilot, Bud Armstrong, informed us that at one crossing ahead of us on the Cimarron there was a saline deposit so strong that one outfit lost more than a hundred cattle which died from drinking the briny waters. The Chisholm Trail had avoided that crossing, but now southern Kansas, due north of us, had been settled so thickly with homesteaders that we would be forced to abandon the old trail and detour to the west. We would have to recross to the south side of the Cimarron at the Saline Reservation, where the waters were the worst. When we reached that ford, we must stampede the herd and run the cattle across the river without permitting them to drink.

Mr. Arnett was much relieved by the arrival of Bud Armstrong and gave him full authority to conduct the outfit. This move soon restored order and discipline in the camp. After nearly four days of trailing on the north side of the Cimarron, through a poor sandy region wooded with a straggling forest of oaks, we came to the Saline Reservation, where we were to recross the river without permitting a single animal to drink from the briny waters.

Armstrong now had us round up our cattle into a compact herd on the north side. We must then get them into a swift stampede before they reached the water's brink. This feat we accomplished by whooping at them as we fought them with our slickers and whipping them with ropes until they were fully stampeded. Now we turned them directly across the stream. Then we had to frighten them on. Since the water at that time was shallow and the river bed was sandy, we had no great trouble in crossing at full speed. But once we were across, our troubles began. The thirsty animals tried to turn back, and it was night before we got them a mile from the river. They were nearly famished. All night long they tried to escape to the river to drink. We had little rest that night. The stench from the putrid bodies of more than a hundred cattle warned us of the danger in allowing our cows to drink from the deadly waters.

Keeping at a safe distance from the deadly stream, with its wide channel resembling a field of snow from the salt crystals upon the dry sand, we came on the following day to Buffalo Creek, a freshwater tributary of the Cimarron. There we found abundant fresh water for our famished cattle and horses. Since the pasturage was good, we decided to rest a day to recruit our animals after this hard experience.

While we were resting on the following day, a small band of Pawnee Indians came to us with the usual requisition for beef. Their leader wore with pride a big copper medal.

"Me love white man heap," he insisted. "Me been after Kiowa Indian. He steal me pony. Kiowa bad Indian, heap. Kiowa want me to help him fight white man. Me tell him no, me love white man. Me tell him Kiowa been a fool. Mebbe-so Kiowa kill one white man. Ten white men come and mebbe-so Kiowa kill ten white man. Mebbe-so Indians kill hundred white man. Me tell Kiowa then thousand white man come and kill every damn Kiowa! Indian can no stop white man. Mebbe-so Indian dam up Red River. Mebbe-so Red River stop running one day. Mebbe-so he stop running two days. Then water get up so big he wash Indian's dam all off."

After this eloquent speech, Mr. Arnett could not refuse the request of the Pawnee. A yearling steer was given him for his great love for the white man.

On the same afternoon, a cloud of dust up the trail indicated that we were about to have another visitor. We soon saw approaching a carriage drawn by a pair of splendid livery horses. To our astonishment, Tom Snyder stepped out of the carriage and began shaking hands with his cowboys. He had come south from Dodge City, now only about 150 miles north of us, to inform Mr. Arnett that he had sold three hundred steers to be delivered at Fort Supply to the Indian agency there. The government in those days bought great numbers of beeves to feed the reservation Indians. We were instructed the next day to cut out all the beeves over four years old until we could fill the contract. We halted our journey until this work could be accomplished, and then we must wait until the detachment of cowboys sent to the reservation with the beeves could return.

The whole procedure required about three days. We spent one day cutting out the cattle and starting them off to Fort Supply, which was about twenty-five miles to the southwest.

Four men were sent with the cattle. Their departure left our outfit so short that we had to do guard duty with only one man left on herd at night. No more were needed to guard the slumbering bovines, but it was lonesome in an Indian country to ride alone for several hours in the darkness, not knowing but that some treacherous savage might want your scalp. Mr. Snyder and his driver left for Dodge City as soon as the beeves were cut out. Bud Armstrong also left in their company. Mr. Arnett had so recovered as to be able to resume his duties as foreman.

After the detachment had left for Fort Supply with the beeves, we were visited by another squad of Indians. They were not as agreeable as the Pawnees. As usual, they demanded a beef, and they did so in an insolent way. Mr. Arnett offered them a crippled yearling, but they indignantly refused it. Their leaders could speak a little Spanish, and our Mexicans served as interpreters. The Indians were informed that they could get nothing, and they were invited to leave. But they did not seem disposed to take their departure. For some time they insisted on the gift of a fat steer. At last, after Mr. Arnett remained firm in his refusal, they rode sullenly away. They were Cheyennes, who were said to be the most treacherous of all Indians. Their visit did not contribute anything to the pleasure of doing guard duty alone that night. When I was called to go on herd after midnight, I carefully armed myself with a good revolver, having exchanged weapons with one of the boys who went to Fort Supply and who wanted my Winchester to shoot antelopes.

I rode silently around the sleeping cattle for several hours, then I was startled by the howl of a wolf to my right. This cry was responded to by another on my left. The howling of wolves on the plains was nothing unusual, but after the

43

quarrel with the Cheyennes, I thought of the Indian tales I had read and of how Indians mimicked the cries of beasts in giving signals for attacks on unsuspecting foes. I kept my weapon ready for any emergency. The cries of the wolves became more frequent and approached nearer. Finally I made out in the starlight the form of an animal a short distance from the herd. I made a dash for it and found it to be a real wolf, after which I fired several shots, greatly accelerating its flight. After that, I felt secure. The wolves were real, and I had nothing to fear from them.

When the boys returned from Fort Supply, we resumed the trail, heading for the Cimarron River.

IV

On the Kansas Plains

WE CROSSED THE CIMARRON again right at the line of Kansas. We were informed that this was the last water we should find until we reached the Arkansas at Dodge City, more than a hundred miles away. The waters of the Cimarron were good at this point, and we watered our herd freely before starting the long drive. We filled our water barrel to the brim, but we started out for a hundred miles without stock water. We had not been averaging more than twelve miles a day, but now we must exceed that rate or our animals would die of thirst before we could reach the Arkansas.

Four days later, on the glorious Fourth of July, we came in sight of the Arkansas River. We had lost no cattle, but they were staggering along in a line for at least five miles up and down the trail. The stronger had outtraveled the weaker, and the herd was pulled in two, forming two distinct droves. Fortunately, there had been showers in the Arkansas Valley south of Dodge City, forming small ponds that enabled the cattle gradually to slake their thirst before they reached the river. Otherwise, we might have lost some cattle from overdrinking.

45

During the time that Mr. Arnett was disabled, there had been a serious difficulty between some of our men and the two Mexicans, which nearly resulted in a shooting affray. Having reduced the number of our cattle by the delivery of three hundred beeves at Fort Supply, we did not need so many hands, and, to prevent further trouble, Mr. Arnett decided to discharge the Garcías at Dodge City. They were tired of the trip and were more than willing to quit. So the chili-eaters, as some cowboys called them, were permitted to resign. Presenting a letter of credit from Mr. Snyder, Mr. Arnett procured the money to pay their wages, and on July 5, I was sent with them to the Atchison, Topeka and Santa Fe station, where they bought tickets to Galveston. I then returned to camp, fording the Arkansas River at the old cow trail.

We now got into trouble through ignorance of Kansas customs. We had never traveled in a country with herd laws. Not dreaming that any men would try to grow a crop of grain without fencing his land, we let our whole herd of 1,700 cattle invade the wheat field of a homesteader. He drove us out with dogs and lurid oaths, but when he was informed of our ignorance, he laughed and said he would excuse us this time but that we must not repeat the experiment.

We bought a fresh supply of provisions at Dodge City, including a keg of pickles. During the entire trip we had tasted no vegetables other than beans or "prairie strawberries" as some called them, and when the pickles were opened, the men would eat nothing else until they were all devoured.

Dodge was said to be the wickedest town in the West at that time, but we saw little of its wickedness. Our stay in town was limited to a few hours each, and that during the day. No cowpuncher was permitted to stay in town at night. Among the curiosities I saw at the station were great piles of buffalo bones awaiting shipment. They were enormous, with the skulls of many of the big bulls still decorated with the short, thick horns peculiar to the buffalo.

[With the arrival of the Atchison, Topeka and Santa Fe Railway in September, 1872, Dodge City became the principal Kansas market for buffalo hides and, a few years later, the state's chief cattle market. By 1879 the Kansas buffaloes had nearly all been killed, and thrifty farmers were gathering and selling the bones. At that time the saloons, bawdy houses, and crime in Dodge had made it known as the Gomorrah of the West. When the Snyder outfit arrived at Dodge, the town had just celebrated the Fourth with a band concert. Recent rains had made the grass green and thick, filled the buffalo wallows, and set the Arkansas River on a boom. Sheriff William Barclay (Bat) Masterson had gone to Leavenworth to deliver a convicted thief to the penitentiary, but Marshal Charles E. Bassett and his assistants, James Masterson and Wyatt Earp, were trying to keep a lid on crime.]

After our shopping was done, we forded the Arkansas River and kept well to the north through western Kansas. The plains were high now, and all watercourses flowed through deep canyons. There were scattered settlements made by homesteaders. The settlers lived chiefly in dugouts, excavations in the sides of canyons, with roofs thatched with grass and then covered with turf. Sometimes we saw houses built of prairie sod as it was turned by the plow and cut in sections like building stones. We were told that in these semi-arid regions sod houses lasted for years.

On one occasion, as we were guiding our weary herd along the trail, the big steers that always led the herd saw a heap of earth and ran bellowing to it. They began to paw it with their forefeet and to toss the turf with their horns. We were unaware that they were destroying a human habitation until a woman came running out from an opening in the ground and fighting the steers frantically with her sunbonnet. When she called on us to drive the cattle away, we hastened to the rescue, but it was too late. The roof of the dugout was caved in and the frontier home ruined. Again we pleaded ignorance, but with no more success than at Dodge City. The woman was greatly exasperated by the partial destruction of her dugout. We offered our services to help rebuild it, but she disdainfully declined them, declaring that persons who were so ignorant as to allow their cattle to destroy the dugout could do little toward repairing it. We were extremely sorry, but we could not gain her forgiveness.

Passing on, we were met by a band of homesteaders mounted on mules and brood mares, all bareback and some barefoot. They approached us in a body and informed us that we must turn to the west, as they had settled on the trail directly north from us and would not allow any Texas cattle to be driven through their settlement. Texas fever, they declared, scattered Texas-fever germs, and the fever would kill their domestic cattle. There was no alternative but to yield to their wishes. We were not prepared to make a forcible invasion of Kansas but must do as directed. So, turning out of our trail, we made a detour of about fifteen miles to go around this settlement.

Not far from this place we found a lone herder running a trail hospital. From several herds, crippled and disabled cattle had been cut out into a hospital bunch and left with this young man to be cared for until they should be able to travel. I was surprised to find that the lonely herder was my old neighbor, Nicholas Branch of Bagdad, Williamson County, Texas. Nick Branch was noted for his faithfulness in every position in which he was placed. I had always admired this trait of his character, but I did not envy him the responsibility of serving as nurse to a drove of lame cattle. He had several horses at his disposal, and he probably arranged with some squatter for his board.

A little farther on, we saw a pathetic scene on the trail. Beside the carcass of a dead horse was a newly made grave. An examination showed that the animal had been killed by lightning. Evidently the thunderbolt had carried instant death to both horse and rider. There was no one to explain, but no explanation was needed. Some Texas cowboy on duty had cashed in—had been killed by lightning and was buried beside the body of his faithful horse. Wolves had nearly devoured the animal's carcass but had not molested the cowboy's grave. There on the wild plains of western Kansas he had been buried, without a woman's tears, without a single tribute of flowers, and doubtless without a coffin. Perhaps a slicker was his only winding sheet. We never learned anything of his history, but here was a solemn admonition to the cowboy that death lurked in the storms that swept over the plains with vivid flashes of lightning.

We now crossed the Kansas Pacific Railroad at Buffalo Parks station, noted as the place where two bandits of the famous Big Springs train robbery had been killed less than two years earlier. They were trying to escape with their booty from Big Springs, Nebraska, when they were killed in a fight with United States troops. In company with Sam Bass, who later was killed by Texas Rangers at Round Rock, Texas, where he planned to rob a bank, and with three other desperadoes, they had stopped the Union Pacific express at Big Springs. They looted the express car, making a rich haul of sixty thousand dollars in twenty-dollar gold pieces being shipped east from California.

[The train robbery at Big Springs, on the evening of September 18, 1877, was perpetrated by six brigands led by Joel Collins. In addition to the gold pieces from the express car, the bandits took several thousand dollars from passengers. Eight days later Collins and Bill Heffridge were killed while resisting arrest.]

On the afternoon of the first day after leaving Buffalo Parks station, we met a man riding across the plain, stopping at intervals to survey the horizon with a field glass. His movements excited our curiosity, and when he came up to us and asked whether we had seen any Indians, we became deeply interested. He said it was rumored that the Cheyennes had left their reservation at Fort Supply in the Indian Territory and had gone on the warpath. It was said that they were following the cow trail to their hunting grounds in Dakota. The rumor further credited them with having killed and scalped a number of settlers in western Kansas. We knew that during the summer of 1878, just one year before, the Cheyennes had made a raid through Kansas and Nebraska, massacring many homesteaders. Later in the afternoon we met several more scouts who told the same story as the lone horseman.

Just before sunset we entered a deep canyon through which flowed a small stream which we were told was a tributary of the Republican River. While we were selecting a camping spot for the night, another scout arrived, claiming to have recent news. He said that the Cheyennes in a large body had crossed the railroad just west of Buffalo Parks on the preceding night and that they were headed north. They must be hiding in some of the deep canyons in our immediate vicinity. He cautioned us to look out for a

50

raid that night. We found some dry driftwood along the creek, and for the first time in many weeks we built a big wood fire by which to eat our evening meal. The cattle had been bedded down about a quarter of a mile farther up the canyon, and three men were guarding them.

As we were quietly eating our supper, these three cowboys dashed up to our camp and said that a large body of horsemen, presumably Indians, were crossing the canyon just above our camp. George Arnett sprang to his feet and called for three volunteers to go with him to reconnoiter. Poinsett Barton, Dick Russell, and I joined him. Arming ourselves, we rode quietly by the dim starlight to the sleeping cattle, then beyond them to the west for half a mile, but we saw no man. We rode up the steep canyon walls to the level plain and halted while Mr. Arnett, who was an old Indian fighter, dismounted and put his ear to the ground. He heard the distant tramping of a large body of horses. We all dismounted then and scanned the horizon of the level plain.

Silhouetted against the northern sky, we saw what appeared to be a large body of horses, or horsemen, rapidly receding in the distant gloom. They might be renegade savages, but if so they had passed us and it would be madness to pursue them. So we followed the rim of the canyon until we were opposite our campfire. Just as we turned to descend, we heard the sound of horses' hoofs and we saw the dim outline of a man on horseback chasing our saddle horses. "Don't shoot!" shouted Mr. Arnett as one of our number brought his carbine to bear on the rider. "I think it's Al Cochran driving the horses." On returning to camp, we found that he was right. The boy had driven the horses up to the wagon.

After reporting the result of our reconnaissance, Mr.

51

Arnett said, "Now, boys, I don't think there is a particle of danger tonight, for the strangers, whoever they are, have crossed the creek and are rapidly leaving us. They will not return. But if any of you are uneasy, we can safely leave the herd and the wagon and go up the canyon a mile or so and remain concealed for the night. The cattle will not run off, and there are no range cattle to mix with them. If no Indians come, the cattle and horses will be safe. If they do come in such force as reported, we shall be powerless to resist them. I do not believe all these Indian tales, but I leave it to you as to what we shall do tonight."

After some discussion, during which I could not help recalling some of Aunt Ellen's stories of Indian massacres, we took a vote and, by an overwhelming majority, decided to leave camp for the night. So we replenished the campfire and filed quietly away on our night horses up the canyon of the creek. Finding a secluded spot hedged in by wild currant bushes, we dismounted and placed a sentinel on guard at the top of the canyon's side. We staked our horses with their saddles on. At regular intervals during the night the sentinel was relieved of his picket duty. Nothing disturbed the silence on the plain during the night except the occasional howl of a coyote.

On the following morning we returned to camp, where we found nothing molested. The cattle had scattered a little, but soon we had them rounded up and ready for the trail. There was no trace of savages. After breakfast we resumed our march up the trail. We soon came to a trail leading to the garrison at Oberlin. It was lined with homesteaders and their families, all in a state of panic from the Indian tales. Some of the women and girls were weeping and some were laughing, but all were flying for their lives to get within the shelter of the soldiers' guns at Oberlin. Scouts were riding over the plains with field glasses, trying in vain to locate the Indians. For several days the panic continued. As we approached the dugouts of the homesteaders, we found them deserted. We no longer had any trouble from settlers who might try to turn us away from our course. No one molested us. In fact, the people seemed glad for our presence. But where were the bloodthirsty Cheyennes?

At last we came to the south prong of Sappa River. There, grazing in the valley, was a herd of about eight hundred horses and a full outfit of cowboys herding them. The outfit was from Texas, and the horses were being trailed to Ogallala, Nebraska, to supply the demand for cow ponies on the big ranches. The boss of the horse herd approached us with a bland smile. After exchanging greetings, he asked, "Seen any Indians?"

"No," we replied, "but we have heard of them every day. What does all this mean?"

"Well," said the horse driver, "we were so harassed by the settlers driving us from place to place that we had to resort to some expedient to make us welcome intruders. They would not let us pass through their settlements and would not let us rest to graze our horses, so we had to do something. We began making night drives and putting out Indian reports. The raid of last year was fresh in memory, and all we had to do to depopulate the plains was to start Indian tales. In our night drives during the dark of the moon, we were mistaken for a strong band of Cheyennes. We are the only Indians in western Kansas, but please keep mum. If they get onto our joke, they will come back and hang us every one. We passed your herd one night on the north prong of the Solomon River. Did you take us for Indians, too?"

It was all plain to us now. We were innocent of the trickery, but we had shared in the benefits of the panic. The unscrupulous old frontiersman who bossed the horse herd knew the source of that hospitality characteristic of border inhabitants when there is danger of savage foes. He had succeeded in making himself welcome by exciting the gravest fears among people unused to the dangers of frontier life. They were all settlers from the East and were easily thrown into a panic by a suggestion of Indians. He had resorted to a heroic treatment for selfishness and had worked a marvelous cure. But, as he said, the secret must be kept until he was at a safe distance from the victims of this faked scare.

V

Bound for Cheyenne

———————◆———————

WE NOW LEFT KANSAS, crossed the southern boundary of Nebraska, and came to the deep canyons through which flow the Republican River and the Frenchman's River. As we approached a canyon, it was a strange spectacle to see the foremost cattle disappear suddenly from the level plain as they descended the steep sides of one of those deep gashes in the earth's surface. Upon the plain there is no slope to indicate the approach to the canyons through which flow the watercourses of that region, and the leaders of our herd seemed to go into the ground just as a prairie dog enters its burrow. Soon the entire herd had disappeared from our view.

We had enjoyed fine weather for more than a month in western Kansas, but now we had a series of thunderstorms. These electric displays came at night, and often with scarcely any precipitation. Usually there was enough rain to wet the polished horns of the Texas Longhorns in a herd, and their acting as reflectors for the lightning gave rise to the delusion that the lightning played upon the cattle's horns. On such occasions all profanity among the cowpunchers ceased. The man who would swear when the lightning danced on the cows' horns was regarded as a Jonah by the outfit, and one inviting the destruction threatened by the elements.

As we approached the Platte River Valley, the country became more broken. We had attained an altitude of about four thousand feet, and an appreciable difference in the density of the atmosphere was noticeable since we had started on our long drive at a little above sea level. Although it was late in July, the nights were cold. The heat was intense at noon, but after sunset radiation was so rapid that we were chilled before dawn.

At last we beheld to the north a long line of silver, which we were informed was the South Platte River. It was many miles away, and on its northern bank trains were seen running east and west. They were on the main line of the Union Pacific, the only great transcontinental railroad at that time.

Just south of Ogallala, we took about four hundred yearlings into our herd through a purchase made by Mr. Snyder. Two of our men, Will and Dick Russell, brothers, decided to return to Texas from Ogallala. Their places were filled by strangers from the East, who were called Shorthorns in the vernacular of the trail to distinguish them from the real Texas cowboy, who was known as a Longhorn.

While we were encamped on the south bank of the Platte, we encountered the most terrific wind and hail storm that I ever experienced. I thought the hail would beat me to death, and the wind blew a hurricane. There was no shelter from the fury of the storm, but fortunately there were no trees on those arid plains to fall upon us. Our cattle drifted about five miles away from the river during the storm, and it required the greater part of the following day to round them up and drive them back to the ford.

Although the Platte was one of those muddy streams that

cowboys called "too thick to drink and too thin to plow," it was a beautiful sight to see the cattle fording it. The river was about a mile wide but was shallow, not coming above the knees of the smallest yearling in the herd. After spending some time in the town of Ogallala, we turned directly to the west and followed the tracks of the Union Pacific along the South Platte River. At Big Springs station we were shown the place where the great train robbery had taken place nearly two years earlier.

While we were grazing our cattle along the railroad between Big Springs and Julesburg, Colorado, one day, the train stopped on the prairie and an elderly gentleman stepped off. Calling to me, he motioned to me to ride nearer.

"Are these Tom Snyder's cattle?" he asked.

"Yes, sir," said I.

"Then lend me your horse to ride to the camp. I am his brother, Dudley H. Snyder of Georgetown, Texas."

"Certainly," I replied as I dismounted and handed him the bridle rein.

He rode away and left me to walk around the herd. I learned that night that he was looking out of the car window for our herd when he recognized the road brand on the cattle. At his request, the train was stopped for him to alight. He had come to inform our foreman that the cattle had been sold to Swan Brothers of Cheyenne and that we were to deliver them at a ranch about twenty miles north of the capital of Wyoming. After arranging all the preliminaries for the delivery of the cattle, he asked me to lend him my night horse to ride to Julesburg that night to catch his train for Cheyenne. After supper he rode away alone to Julesburg.

On the next morning I rode in the wagon to that town, where I found my horse picketed out near the station.

Julesburg was a mere hamlet in the northeast corner of Colorado. At that point we left the Platte Valley and followed the old Mormon Trail up the valley of Lodge Pole Creek, soon re-entering Nebraska.

The rise of the Mormon Church was an illustration of the power of persecution as a church builder. Persecution drove the Mormons from place to place until, in June, 1844, their prophet, Joseph Smith, was mobbed and murdered at Nauvoo, Illinois. From the day of that murder, their increase was assured. In 1847, thirty-two years prior to our trip along the same trail, they had marched across the continent under the leadership of Brigham Young and founded their settlement at Salt Lake, Utah. As we trailed our weary cattle over the same route for about one hundred miles, we saw everywhere evidences of their desperate journey. At intervals along the trail were neglected graves of victims of Indian massacres and of others who had died of exposure and fatigue upon that dreadful trail. Here and there were still to be found parts of some of their handcarts that had been abandoned. Chipping one of them with my pocketknife, I found that it was built of cypress. The wood was perfectly preserved to that day.

[Unable to buy wagons and horses such as those used by earlier Mormon pioneers, several thousand started on a trip of nearly 1,400 miles across the plains and mountains in 1856, hauling their belongings on handcarts. Many of them were recent European immigrants, unused to the hardships of the frontier. Their trip was marked by hardship, horror, and a tragic death toll.]

There is something in the human heart that makes one admire the man or woman who dies for his or her faith, be that faith full of error. There usually is someone to carry on the work of a martyr. Brigham Young, in espousing the

58

cause of Joseph Smith, discovered a field for his powers as an organizer and as a ruler of great executive ability. In the desert he founded for a time an empire of religious despotism that will immortalize his name. Persecution did for his sect what the Spanish Inquisition did for the Protestant faith. It built up a denomination that today has its missionaries seeking converts over the entire civilized world.

We now came to Sidney, Nebraska, a typical frontier town full of cowboys, adventurers, explorers, and hunters. Here we procured some elk meat from a local butcher and found it to be excellent. On the shambles of a local market we saw exposed for sale prairie chickens, antelope meat, venison, bear meat, and specimens of every other kind of game known in the region. Hunting was not restricted then by game laws, and everyone killed as many wild animals as he wished, selling the meat as he pleased. The hunter's license had not yet been dreamed of in those parts.

Following the course of Lodge Pole Creek, we now came to Pine Bluffs, the gateway to Wyoming. Here, between two cliffs covered with a growth of pines, we passed into Wyoming Territory. We would now leave the Union Pacific Railroad and bear to the north to reach the ranch on Horse Creek where we were to deliver our cattle. Pine Bluffs was an important center where thousands of fat cattle were shipped during each summer to Eastern packeries. It was the shipping point for nearly all the ranches in southern Wyoming. Cheyenne was the chief town of the region, but the little village of Pine Bluffs was given preference because of its superior facilities for getting forage to beeves on their way to market.

Here we Texas cowboys learned something about handling cattle for the market. We were rough in our treatment of the animals. It had never occurred to us that cattle had

59

nerves or that they lost weight from being constantly frightened. Watching the careful handling of the fat cattle brought to Pine Bluffs for the Chicago market, we were astonished at the kind, gentle treatment of every animal. If a steer strayed from the herd, he was gently coaxed back, whereas we were accustomed to chasing him back at full speed. Rough handling, the local men explained, caused the beef to lose weight. No shipper, they said, would tolerate for a single day a cowpuncher who was so foolish as to make his steers run at full speed.

As we left the valley of Lodge Pole Creek, we came upon a high plateau, a part of that upon which stands the Rocky Mountain range. We learned that we had now attained an altitude of six thousand feet above sea level. From this elevation we could see the tops of the snow-capped peaks of the mountains above North Park, Colorado, more than a hundred miles away. The haze of the atmosphere through which they were viewed at that distance gave the snowy peaks a rich, creamy color resembling that of the yellowish thunderheads seen sometimes at a great distance in Texas. One lofty summit which rose above its neighbors was pointed out as Long's Peak. I feasted my eyes for several days on the backbone of America. Sometimes a bank of clouds would obscure the peaks. A storm was raging in the mountains, I was told.

We had reached the great plateau about August 12. The nights were extremely chilly to us Texans. We had traveled so slowly up the trail, however, that we suffered little more than did the residents. Crossing the continent at the rate of ten or twelve miles a day does not subject the traveler to the sudden changes brought about nowadays by going from Texas to Wyoming in a day and a night by rail. We became acclimated as we went.

60

One afternoon as we were grazing our cattle upon the elevated plains, Will Bower borrowed my Winchester to shoot at some antelopes he saw not far away. He soon returned, dragging a mother antelope he had shot. We now had steak for supper. On the following morning I saw some antelopes in the same direction and went out on foot with my carbine. In order to approach as near as possible, I crawled for some distance through the grass. As I drew near the spot, I arose to my feet to find that all had fled except two kids that seemed to have no fear of man as they ran toward me, bleating as if calling their mother. I could not shoot the poor little creatures when they reposed so much confidence in me. I turned and retraced my steps toward the camp. On the way back, I found and shot a large rattlesnake.

We came at last, on August 15, to the point where we were to deliver the cattle to the purchasers. Swan Brothers of Cheyenne sent a foreman with a complete outfit of cowboys to take charge. To them we delivered all of the cattle except a few work oxen that were sold to another party.

[The Swan brothers, Alexander H., Thomas, and Henry, with Henry's son, Will F., had come to Wyoming from Iowa in 1873 and formed the Swan Brothers Cattle Company. In 1880, Henry and Will sold out to Alex and formed their own company. Three years later, with Scotch capital, Alex established the Swan Land and Cattle Company, of which he became manager. In May, 1887, after severe cattle losses in the blizzards of the preceding winter, the Swan empire crashed. The announcement of its failure, wrote John Clay, "fell like a bombshell in Cheyenne, and the cattle industry of the West was shaken to its foundation."]

Our saddle horses were sold to a third party, and they,

61

with the oxen, must be taken to Cheyenne with us. I had brought up the trail a good young mare that was my own property, and I decided to sell her in Cheyenne.

Cheyenne was a frontier town of perhaps 15,000 people. The capital of Wyoming Territory, it had two railroads, one leading south to Denver and the Union Pacific running east and west from Ogden, Utah, to Omaha, Nebraska. After five months of rough life on the trail, we Texas cowboys, deprived as we had been of all the conveniences and comforts of civilization, were a picturesque squad as we rode into Cheyenne. Our neglected and dilapidated clothes were worn and patched, our hair was uncut, and our faces unshaven. We presented no particularly novel sight to the natives, however, as they were accustomed to the arrival of travel-worn cowboys.

At Cheyenne we delivered the oxen to some freighters who were running a trail of wagons from Cheyenne to Deadwood, Dakota, and other remote places. The wagonmaster who received the oxen took them at once to a blacksmith shop to be shod. To see shoes put on oxen was a novel sight to us Texans. First each animal was hogged down and two plates of steel were nailed to each foot. Then each toe of the animal had to have a separate plate or shoe.

We had not drawn anything on our wages during the entire trip. After we reached the city, we went to a bank where Mr. Arnett procured the cash to pay us off. Now we must buy clothes and assume the appearance of civilians. Almost the first man I met in the street was Landrum Poole, a neighbor from Liberty Hill. Landy, as he was called, had preceded us with another herd, and, having been several days in Cheyenne, he knew where to get just what we wanted in clothing. Under his guidance we bought complete outfits. We next repaired to barber shops, where we were trimmed before cleaning up and donning our new clothes. After undergoing such changes that we did not recognize one another, we again appeared on the street. Our next task was to find a place to stay.

A number of us went with Mr. Arnett to the Metropolitan Hotel. Our abode at that hostelry was short-lived, however. The next morning at breakfast a big Negro came in the dining room and took the chair next to Mr. Arnett as he sat at breakfast. It had been only fourteen years since the close of the Civil War, and race prejudice was still strong. Mr. Arnett, unfortunately, did not take time to protest. He merely arose and smashed his chair over the head of the Negro. The latter uttered a great outcry, which soon brought a policeman. He arrested Mr. Arnett and took him off to court, where he was heavily fined for the assault. The proprietor told us that he was unable to discriminate against Negro guests, as the Civil Rights bill had recently been enacted by Congress and the Territory of Wyoming was directly under federal control.

On the streets that day I met many cowboys from Texas. They confirmed the statement of our host that not a hotel in the city would turn away a Negro if he had the money to pay for his room and meals. Among those I met was Sam Moses of Burnet County, a son of Captain Norton Moses, one of the most distinguished citizens of Texas. Sam was staying in a private boarding house where no Negroes were entertained. He took me to that place, and we had no more trouble.

Mr. Arnett and several of our men left in a few days for their homes in Texas. The others of us had decided to see more of Wyoming before returning. One day I met John Snyder, another brother of my employer, Tom Snyder. John Snyder was then manager of a big cattle ranch for

Mrs. J. W. Iliff, a wealthy widow who had some fine ranch property in Wyoming. He said he would try to find a temporary job for me, and together we went to the office of the Swan brothers. They wanted three men to join an outfit trailing a herd of cattle to a ranch they owned near Fort Fetterman on the North Platte River.

After promising to find two other good hands, I looked up Albert Cochran and Poinsett Barton, who were still in town. They agreed to go, and the next day we reported to the Swans for duty. Horses were assigned, and we were placed in charge of John Winterling, our foreman for the trip. His other men were all Shorthorns.

As the ranch from which we were to start was twenty-five miles out, we started out there at once. Winterling and his men led the way. Our horses were fast and were superior to the poor ponies we had ridden up the trail from Texas. As soon as we were out of Cheyenne, Winterling set out across the plains and signaled us to follow. He started off at a brisk gallop, but we thought he would soon slow down. To our surprise he kept up this gait for the whole twenty-five miles. It was the hardest ride I had ever taken, as I was not used to running a horse for half a day without a stop. At last we arrived at the ranch, more dead than alive.

The ranch where we received the cattle was on the banks of Horse Creek, a tributary of the North Platte River. There we found our chuck wagon and other equipment awaiting us. A man named Cody, who was foreman of the ranch, delivered the cattle, about five hundred head, to be trailed to La Bonte. We bedded the cattle on the plains that night and, on the following morning, took our posts in trailing them north over the Cheyenne and Deadwood road.

Every few miles along this route was a roadhouse, a small grocery store where supplies, including cigars and liquor, were sold. Nothing was priced at less than twenty-five cents. This meant that a cigar or the smallest drink was a quarter.

On the second night from the ranch our boss and his Shorthorn cowboys tarried too long at a roadhouse and became hilarious. Barton, Cochran, and I remained sober and had all the herd duty to perform until our friends sobered up. But that was not difficult, and we did not mind the work.

On this trail we often met wagon trains from Deadwood and other mining towns off the railroad. Each train was made up of several ox teams of twelve oxen to the team. With each team was a driver. Frequently three or four wagons were fastened together and were drawn by one team of sixteen to twenty oxen. With each team was a herd of extra oxen and two men, one to herd during the day and the other at night. The night herder slept in one of the wagons during the day. One cook presided over the culinary art for the train, and the whole outfit was under a wagonmaster or foreman.

The oxen were never necked together as was the custom in Texas. When they were unyoked from the wagon, they were turned loose into the common night herd to graze on the plain. A few saddle horses were taken along for use of the wagonmaster and the herders. Since the trails were stony, the oxen were shod with steel. A few of the wagons were drawn by mules instead of oxen, but those were exceptions.

When we came to the headwaters of Chugwater Creek, we followed its meanderings along the foot of the Laramie Mountains to the Laramie River. There we saw an unusual feat of road building in the mountains. The Laramie River was bridged by building large triangular pens of long pine logs for piers upon which to rest the stringers. Each pen had the apex of the triangle pointed upstream to offer as little resistance as possible to the current. Then the pen was filled with boulders, giving it the weight of solid masonry. Upon these pens the long wooden bridge was built.

When we reached the river, the water was so low that no bridge was needed. After fording the Laramie, we entered a broken, rocky region amid the foothills of the Laramie range. In the streams we often saw beaver dams that formed large ponds. Lining the banks of the ponds were the stumps of trees that the beavers had gnawed down. Some of the work was recent, showing that the beavers were cutting trees every night.

Soon after we had crossed the Laramie River, we came to Cottonwood Creek, named for the trees that lined its banks. It was a typical mountain stream with a fine flow of pure water from the melting snow on the mountains. In the bottom just below the ford we heard the baying of a pack of hounds. Then came the report of a big gun. Some of our men went to see what was happening.

They soon returned, bringing with them the front half of a grizzly bear stripped of its skin, except that the paws and the face were not skinned. The hunter who had just killed the bear, not wanting anything but the skin and the hams, had given us the remainder. Part of it was cooked for our supper. It tasted much like fresh pork, but I could not enjoy it, since the face and paws of the grizzly, in view before me near the camp, had such a human appearance that I felt like a cannibal.

In a mountain gorge through which we passed, we saw a flock of that peculiar species of pheasant, the sage hen. The birds were large, many of them larger than the domestic fowl. They were gentle and showed little fear of the men. We did not shoot any of the sage hens, since we were told that their meat was not edible. Because they fed on the sagebrush that covered the foothills, their flesh was said to taste so strongly of sage that it was nauseating.

In one of the gorges I saw some pine stumps that had been cut with an ax twenty feet above the ground. I was told that they had been cut in the winter when the gorge was full of snow. The woodsman merely stood on the drift snow and cut the trees where they stuck out of it.

Here the mountains were covered with a thick growth of pine nearly to their summits. One evening as we were eating supper, an excited man on horseback came galloping to us. One of our party, a local ranchman, hailed him and asked, "What's the matter?"

"I've set the reservation on fire," he said.

"How did it happen?" we asked.

"I was cutting wood on the timber reservation when fire from my camp got into the pine straw. Now the whole timber reservation is aflame."

The poor wretch was flying from arrest and punishment for his carelessness. Turning to the direction from which he came, we could see that the entire mountainside was afire. Occasionally the flames would leap to the top of a pine, lighting the countryside for miles. All night the flames raged in the forest among the mountains. But we were told that this reservation was not a large one and that the forest rangers would soon bring the fire under control.

When we reached the ranch at La Bonte where we were to deliver the cattle, we were told to stay and brand them before they were turned loose. Among the visitors on our first night there was powerfully built Billy Brown, the son of a white father and a Sioux mother. He boasted that he was the first child born in Denver with white blood in his veins.

After branding the cattle, which did not take long, my companions and I decided to return to the Lone Star State. So we boarded an eastbound Union Pacific train and were on our way back to Texas. After several days of what seemed perfect luxury to a trio of weary cowpunchers, we were happy to be again on the soil of our own state. At Waco we bought horses to take us back to our homes.

At Liberty Hill, I was glad to rejoin Aunt Ellen and other relatives, who were much relieved at my safe return. But as they listened eagerly to my account of the trip, I knew that I should never regret having made a drive up the old Chisholm Trail.

In a few years the trail became a relic of the past. Today neatly plowed furrows of prosperous farms leave little trace of it or of the ranges that bordered it. Great horses of steel now carry thousands of Texas cattle to Northern markets. Huge bridges of steel and concrete stretch across the streams where once waded millions of Texas Longhorns, and thriving villages cover camp grounds that once resounded with stampeding hoofbeats.

Gone are the buffaloes and their hunters. The cowboy has settled down on the ranges to the west. But the memories of the trail driver linger on, like those of the minstrels of old, and many are the tales handed down by the survivors of the great trek to the Northern and Western plains.

Other Frontier Writings

The Regulators

———◆———

IT WAS THE YEAR 1860. A traveler rode up to the house
of Major Ephraim Roddy, six miles north of Lexington,
Texas. Stopping at the back gate, he asked for a drink of
water. Little John Fletcher, the major's grandson, took him
a drink from the well. Joe noticed that the visitor was accompanied by two small Negro boys on another horse.
Slave traders frequently carried slaves on an extra horse
along the public road, and the occurrence caused no com-
ment.

The next morning Joe Roddy, Major Roddy's youngest
son, went early to Lexington on horseback, armed, as was
necessary in those days, with his six-shooter. There he met
Matt Morgan and a stranger in earnest conversation.

"Come here, Joe," said Morgan when he saw Joe. "This
man is from La Grange. He is a deputy sheriff of Fayette
County, and he is hunting a Negro thief who has stolen
two Negro boys from old Colonel Tom Moore down on the
Colorado River. Have you seen anything of such a man
with two Negro boys?"

"No, Captain, I have not," replied Joe. "But my little

nephew saw such a man and gave him a drink of water at my father's gate late yesterday afternoon."

"Then we'll get him," exclaimed Morgan. "Come on, boys," he called to a group of men not far away. "He was here yesterday, and we can overtake him. Joe, will you come along?"

Joe Roddy was always ready for an adventure fraught with danger. "Sure, I'll go," he replied.

As the recognized leader of the Regulators, a term applied in the Old South to men who voluntarily tracked down escaped or stolen slaves, Matt Morgan was famous chiefly for the number of men his mob had hanged. There was Tom Cox, for one victim. Tom Middleton was another. They were numerous and in most cases were criminals, and the country was better off by their having been lynched. Yet some deplored such a means of enforcing the institution of slavery. Major Roddy as a retired attorney had a profound regard for the majesty of the law, and he had impressed on his sons, Baylis and Joe, that every man was entitled to his day in court. Neither boy had ever taken part in a lynching, and Joe did not now anticipate such an occurrence in the presence of the officer from Fayette County. So he joined in the chase of the "Negro thief," a term applied only to white men who stole slaves.

At Major Roddy's, little Joe Fletcher gave the men a minute description of the traveler and the horses, all of which corroborated the officer's description. The men knew they were on the right track, and they rode north all day. The fugitives were heard of frequently along the way, and the pursuers were rapidly gaining on them when night came. The posse camped on the trail that night. Early the next day the horsemen resumed the hunt. Not far from Cameron, near the Little River bottom, Joe Roddy and Pete Martin, who were in the lead, shouted, "Yonder they go!"

The robber looked back and saw he was pursued. Directing the Negroes to take to the bottom to the right, he made a dash for a deep and densely wooded ravine on the left. Roddy and Martin followed the white man, who was the only source of danger, and Morgan and the rest of the posse followed the Negro boys.

It was the trick of Negro thieves to promise freedom to the slaves they stole, so that the latter would assist in the escape. Those promises were "kept" by their selling the slaves to the highest bidder for cash. So the little slaves were desperately in earnest in trying to escape capture.

In the chase after the thief, Roddy, being the better mounted, said, "Drop behind him, Pete, and if he goes to shoot, kill him; but let me try to capture him alive. I'll outrun him and head him off from the ravine."

Roddy easily ran ahead of the fugitive and, throwing his six-shooter in position, commanded a halt. The robber started to turn his horse, but he saw that Martin had the drop on him from the rear. His hands went up, and he begged for mercy. It was granted. He was searched and was found unarmed. If he had had any weapons, he must have thrown them away in his flight. He then begged for protection from mob violence.

When the captors returned to the road, they found the officer and Morgan's men waiting for them. A hangman's noose already had been made with a rope.

"Boys, let's hang him right here," said Morgan, who, like a bloodhound, began to scent human blood.

"Hang him!" all shouted except his captors and the deputy sheriff. The officer made a feeble attempt to subdue the mob spirit, but in vain. Then he gracefully yielded to the inevitable as he saw it. The prisoner looked imploringly at his captors.

Joe Roddy spoke first. "Captain Morgan, Pete and I promised this man that if he would surrender we would protect him, and we can't allow him to be hanged here."

Morgan laughed hoarsely and said, "Joe, you are awful good, but you can't help yourself." Then, turning to his mob, he ordered, "String him up, boys."

The "boys" moved toward the prisoner as if to execute the order of their chief. Then Martin and Roddy rode quickly, one on either side of the trembling thief, and said, as they drew their six-shooters, "We'll die before we'll let you hang this man after we promised to protect him. We'll shoot the first man that touches him."

The would-be lynchers fell back. Morgan and his confederates held a consultation. Then he announced that they would postpone the hanging until they got back to Lexington.

Soon all were mounted and on their way home. Roddy and Martin rode on either side of the prisoner. When they reached Major Roddy's farm, Joe wanted to leave them, but the prisoner begged so hard that he went on to Lexington. There Morgan's mob was large—reinforced by others of the Regulators—and the proposal to lynch was resumed. Again Roddy and Martin interfered. Again it was postponed. Roddy and Martin would not leave the prisoner until Morgan promised not to lynch him before reaching Winchester, and then to leave it to the Fayette County people to vote on his life or death. The told Morgan they would hold him personally responsible for any breach of faith.

Morgan kept faith and saw the prisoner and the little

slaves safely to Winchester, where the owner of the Negroes lived. There the cry for lynching was renewed, but Lytt Moore, a son of the owner, made a speech to the mob, denounced Morgan as a murderer, and finally prevented the lynching. Lytt Moore afterward served as district judge at La Grange and for many years was a member of Congress from his district.

The thief was tried at La Grange for stealing Colonel Tom Moore's Negroes and was convicted and sentenced to the penitentiary, but he was pardoned with others on an agreement to serve in the Confederate Army. There he was lost sight of, but if he survived that conflict he owed his wretched life to the heroism of Joe Roddy and Pete Martin. Martin was killed a few years later in the Confederate Army.

Not long after the Regulator incident Joe Roddy joined the Confederate Army. He served for awhile under Captain Matt Morgan. On one occasion the officers were trying to drill the recruits in guard duty. Roddy's time came to do picket duty. It was a custom among officers to try to catch the pickets off their guard mentally and get a soldier to let the officer look at his gun. Then the officer would arrest him for carelessness and send him to the guardhouse. While Roddy was on picket one night with his Enfield rifle, Captain Morgan came upon him.

"Joe, that looks like a fine gun. Let me see it a minute." Private Roddy handed him the gun. Morgan laughed savagely. Now he would send Joe Roddy, the bold defender of the Negro thief, to the guardhouse. "Fall in line, Joe. Let's go to the guardhouse!" said the captain, laughing.

"Wait a minute," said Joe, as he threw a cocked revolver in the captain's face and added, "Captain Morgan, give me my gun!"

"Ah, Joe, you have that old six-shooter again! Here, take your rifle. I was only joking."

Joe Roddy had taken a desperate chance. He might have been court-martialed. But he knew at heart that Matt Morgan was a coward and was formidable only as a mob leader. Morgan never again annoyed Joe Roddy.

Trailing Comanche Raiders

———◀◆▶———

ONE NOVEMBER MORNING in 1869 my grandmother said to her son: "Joseph, we want some flour for our Thanksgiving dinner. Can't you take some new wheat to Alex Barton's mill and get some of Alex's Best?"

"Yes, Ma," said my uncle, "I'll go right after dinner."

Our dinner was served early that day; the horses were harnessed to our light wagon, some bags of wheat were taken from the granary, a roll of blankets was tossed into the wagon, corn and oats were added for the team, and our provision box completed the load. I was seated on the spring seat when my uncle kissed his mother, sister, wife, and babies good-by and, bringing along his big six-shooter that he gallantly had worn for four years in the Confederate cavalry, joined me, waving adieu to Grandpa.

Our wagon was soon rambling over the white rocks in the bed of sparkling South San Gabriel Creek on our fifteen-mile drive to Cedar Mills, as Alex Barton's place was known. The weather threatened a wet norther; but the mist rolled away, there was a rift in the clouds, and the sun burst forth in a flood of dazzling light upon the beautiful San Gabriel Valley. As we trotted along, we came upon

higher ground. There was a broad expanse of prairie covered with tall yellow grass, then a bright green belt of winter
wheat like a field of emerald set in gold. I was aroused from
a childish reverie by a voice.

"That is Dr. Westfall's place," my uncle was explaining
as we passed a pretty house in the old colonial style. Then,
to our left, we saw Hopewell Church in the distance. At
last we came to the edge of the cedar brakes. Climbing a
steep rocky incline, we landed on a level stretch covered
with thickets of cedar and shin-oak bushes. The ground
was strewn with boulders of rough, honeycombed limestone
in such wild confusion that they seemed to have rained
down—a tempest of stones. As we rambled over this rocky
road, an opening appeared in the cedars to our left. A deep
canyon led off toward the Colorado River. At its bottom a
stream of crystal water glistened like a thread of silver.
Clinging to its walls were evergreen bushes of agarita and
Texas mountain laurel, contrasting beautifully with the
scarlet berries of the sumac and the purple autumn leaves
of the spotted oaks that grew in patches amid the shelving
rocks—and all illuminated by the gorgeous rays of the setting sun. To my childish fancy it seemed like a bit of fairy-
land. You can guess the shock to my imagination when
my uncle exclaimed, "There is the head of Devil's Hollow."

Just then a crackling sound, like the breaking of a dry
stick in the cedars to our right, made old Dan snort and
plunge forward against his traces. Boston, too, took fright
and tried to run. My uncle drew his six-shooter as he reined
the frightened horses. We looked in the direction from
which the sound came but saw only the green cedars and
their brown trunks.

A chaparral cock ran out of a brake and down the road

in front of us. Then, perching on a rock, he uttered one of his peculiar cries of alarm. My uncle raised his revolver to shoot the bird, but, as if appealed to by some sudden thought, he lowered the weapon and the pheasant escaped. The reins being loosened, our horses needed no whip but dashed away as if glad to quit the haunted spot.

Then he saw a clearing to the right. A small field, enclosed with a fence of cedar poles, and a small cedar log cabin occupied the clearing. Two men stood near the cabin, shading their eyes with their hands and gazing in the direction from whence came the sound that had frightened the horses.

"Who lives there?" I asked.

"Old McNew, the hunter," was the reply. My uncle now relapsed into his accustomed silence but drove rapidly on.

A few miles from there another opening appeared in the thick cedar forest. With brakes on, our wagon was soon rumbling, slipping, sliding, and screeching down the steep rocky declivity leading into the village of Cedar Mills. At the head of the valley, near a bold spring, stood Alex Barton's mill, the black smoke from its fire of resinous cedar issuing from a tall rock chimney. Tom Vaughn's store, the post office, a blacksmith shop, and a few cottages with rough rock fences completed the picture. To unload our wheat, camp, feed, and make a fire was the work of but a few minutes. The sun was down, and the full moon had risen as we entered the valley.

As our fire of cedar faggots burned brightly while Uncle Joe prepared supper, Alex Barton, proprietor of the combined sawmill, grist mill, and flour mill, and Tom Vaughn, merchant and postmaster, joined us. They discussed the weather, Reconstruction, wheat prospects, the price of sawed cedar, and kindred topics. Joe Roddy and Alex Barton already were fast friends. Their fathers had been neighbors at Spartanburg, back in the old Palmetto State.

"Joe," asked Alex, "did you come around by McFarland's or straight through the cedar brakes?"

"Through the brakes, Alex, right by the head of Devil's Hollow."

"You ought not to have done it, Joe. It's dangerous in the full of the moon. That's the way Craig got killed—carelessness, traveling in the mountains in the full of the moon. I remember, Joe, about five years ago last July the Indians raided South Gabriel Valley as far down as Taylor Smith's and Johnny Bryson's settlements. Them there Comanches rounded up a big bunch of horses, and right there at Monroe Spencer's spring on Larry Branch, two fine mares they stole from Wash Miller and Johnny Russell broke to run off, and the red devils shot 'em down right there. Next mornin' Ollie Spencer, John Bryan, and Bob Poole found their carcasses stuck full of arrows. From there the red devils went right through Parson Spencer's peach orchard and stole all the peaches they could eat. Might not be any danger now, Joe, but them's good horses you got, and just you and the boy. I wouldn't like—Hello! Who comes there?"

"Howdy, Alex!" shouted the foremost as he reined his steed.

"Why, howdy, Babe. What in the world has happened?"

"Indians!" exclaimed Babe.

"Indians? Where, Babe?"

"In Devil's Hollow."

"When, and how many were seen, Babe?"

"This evenin', about five o'clock. Pap and me seen 'bout fifteen Indians in war paint afoot in the cedar brakes mighty close to home and right at the head of Devil's Hollow. A

80

man and a boy was just ahead of 'em in a two-horse wagon. Pap's 'fraid they was killed and scalped, but these here are the horses, and I believe this is the man and boy."

"By George, Joe, you all had a close shave, didn't you?" said Barton.

"Good night, fellows," said Babe. "We got to go and 'larm the settlements."

Barton detained him, asking, "Babe, where is your pap?" "Gone to 'larm the Hopewell settlement and Buck Elliott and Dr. Westfall. Good night, fellows," and Babe and his companions were off like a shot.

All down the valley we heard the clattering of hoofs as this young Paul Revere and his brother rode away on their brave errand. At each settler's cabin the horsemen shouted: "Indians! Look out for your horses! Indians comin' sure!"

As soon as Babe McNew was gone, we held a council of war. Alex Barton was spokesman.

"I tell you, Joe, there will be no danger till about midnight. Indians on a raid never go through this valley before that time. My mill will run till ten o'clock. Then you can lead your horses in the millhouse and sleep upstairs."

The mill shut down at the appointed time. "Now let's get the horses in the house," said Mr. Barton. But they balked and refused to enter.

"Never mind, Alex," said my uncle. "I will tie them to these posts and sit upstairs and watch."

A pallet was made for me while my protector sat near a door overlooking the horses. I soon fell asleep, but after awhile strange sounds awoke me. There was a commotion in the valley. The distinct tramping of a herd of horses, as they were being driven through a rocky pass, was plainly heard. The dogs were barking at every house.

81

Alarmed, I crawled to where my uncle sat, six-shooter in hand, gazing into the moonlit mill yard.

"What is that noise?" I whispered.

"Hush!" and he motioned me back.

"It's Indians," whispered my companion. "Get back."

I needed no second command but buried my head in the blankets, expecting the battle to open. Not a shot was fired, however, and not an Indian came near the horses. It was the scent of the savages that had made old Dan cut up so.

With the passage of the herd of stolen horses over a mountain trail, driven by the wily Comanches, the noise ceased and all was quiet again at Cedar Mills.

"Well, Joe," said Alex Barton the next day at sunrise, "did you see the Comanches go by?"

"Yes, Alex, they seemed to have a good drove of horses, and I thought once they had old Dan. We'll go back by the prairie route, Alex, and keep out of the cedar brakes."

So we drove home without molestation, meeting Mr. McFarland, who told us he narrowly escaped the loss of all his horses.

Another scene was being enacted not many miles away. All night long the brave McNew boys rode, spreading the news. Other daring spirits joined in arousing the slumbering settlers. Oatmeal Creek, Bear Creek, North San Gabriel, Backbone Valley, Brooksville, the head of Rocky—all were visited by swift couriers, and a pursuit was planned before dawn.

Moses' Ranch was selected as a starting point.

"The Indians are going out with a drove of stolen horses. We must follow them. Bring your guns and meet us at Moses' Ranch by daybreak" was the message flashed by an old system of wireless telegraphy all over Burnet and parts of Williamson counties.

Colonel Norton Moses lived on the heights south of the North San Gabriel Valley. The view from his ranch swept the horizon from Bachelor's Peak, a mere pimple on its northern rim, to Pilot Knob in the east. Colonel Moses was easily the most prominent citizen in that part of the frontier. He was an Indian fighter of no mean reputation. Everybody recognized his courage and sagacity. So it was natural to select his ranch as a recruiting station for an expedition against the Comanches. Then, his place was near the old San Saba trail that bent around the cedar brakes and kept in the open country. In sneaking in to raid the settlements, the savages kept well to the mountains. But when they made a dash to escape with a drove of horses, they were compelled to follow a more feasible route.

Before the first streak of dawn the clans were gathering. Horsemen indifferently mounted on "what was left to ride," some on mules and some on big-bellied brood mares, others on stove-up plow horses, armed with any old firearm of that day but full of fight, came and joined in the council of war.

Colonel Moses and Captain George Arnett were leaders. At daybreak the cavalcade of about fifty men and boys went out to strike the trail. They soon discovered a place where the tall grass was beaten down, and expert trailers said the sign was fresh and undoubtedly the trail of the Indian drive. For some miles the trail was plain and pursuit easy. Then all was blank again.

"It's an old trick of the redskins," said Colonel Moses. "They have stampeded and scattered their herd to throw us off."

Much time was lost in hunting the trail. At last Colonel Moses found a dim trail leading toward Bachelor's Peak, a favorite Indian route. Captain Arnett held the opinion that the Indians would hug the cedar brakes and favored following up the old San Saba trail. The men were divided in opinion as much as the leaders. Things were quickly decided in such emergencies. The forces were divided, so that each leader was to follow his own notion with half of the men. Arnett and his men rode rapidly up the San Saba trail while Colonel Moses and his squad set off across Rocky for Bachelor's Peak.

Captain Arnett kept the trail flanked right and left by his best scouts and trailers. The day was far advanced, and little had been seen to encourage the pursuit. A wagon train was sighted in the distance. Captain Arnett rode rapidly forward to meet it. The train consisted of ten wagons loaded with pecans and dried buffalo meat, a herd of extra mules, a Mexican herder, a cook, a night herder, ten Mexican teamsters, and a wagonmaster. All were heavily armed, and no wandering band of Comanches had any thought of attacking such an outfit. Captain Arnett learned from the herder that no Indians had been seen. The wagonmaster came up and heard the news. Captain Arnett bought some pecans and dried buffalo meat from the train, and soon the hungry men were feasting.

"Los Indios!" shouted a muleteer of the train, causing all eyes to turn where he pointed. No animated thing was in sight, but to the west could be seen a thin white cloud of dust rising from behind a prairie ridge a full mile away from the trail. This was significant.

"Indians!" cried every voice in chorus. Hats full of pecans were emptied on the ground, and scraps of buffalo hump were cast away as each rider seized his bridle reins and dashed away to the pursuit.

When the Texans came to the crest of the next ridge, the Indians were seen rushing their horses over another great

84

prairie billow half a mile away. The pursuers redoubled their efforts to gain on the enemy in crossing the intervening valley. When they again sighted the Indians, not more than four hundred yards intervened. The savages stampeded their stolen herd to the right and sought safety in flight toward the hills on the left, hotly pursued by George Arnett and his men, who began firing as the Indians entered a rocky defile, skirted on each side by thickets of cedar and shin oak. A shot from Arnett's Henry rifle brought one feathered warrior from his horse, but the wounded Comanche escaped in the undergrowth, and no further notice was taken of him.

The Indians, being better mounted and superb horsemen, now kept easily out of range of such weapons as the Texans had. Arnett's men were scattered, according to the speed of their mounts, for half a mile. At last the Indians were seen to dismount suddenly, and turning their horses into a cedar brake, they took shelter behind the rocks at the falls on Morgan's Creek and opened fire for the first time on their pursuers. Their tawny faces were peering over the rocks, and they shouted and yelled exultantly, firing their rifles at the scattered Texans.

They were safe. Their position was as impregnable as Gibraltar. Below the falls, cliffs of rock rose a hundred feet. On each side was a dense cedar brake. They held the only pass and opened fire with Henry rifles as the settlers approached. Arnett fired his carbine at the enemy and, wheeling his horse, rode out of range to await reinforcements.

Here they came, helter-skelter, down the rocky trail—cowboys first, then old men and boys on mares, mules, and stove-ups. Each wheeled and fired his Enfield rifle, six-shooter—whatever he had—as he reached the danger line and rode rapidly back to a point out of range of the enemies' guns. The savages yelled like demons and laughed in defiance at the Texans. Arnett realized that he was beaten. The enemy outnumbered his men, was better armed, and so fortified as to make a fight hopeless. He was brave but was too good a soldier to lead his men into a death trap with small hope of doing the enemy the slightest injury. A red warrior, splendidly mounted on a stolen stallion, sallied from the stronghold and, by gestures and Spanish oaths, defied the settlers. One impetuous youth started to meet him.

"It's no use, Armstead," said Arnett. "Come back. It's certain death for no good. Let's go back and round up the horses and go home."

The drove of stolen horses had not wandered far from where the Indians left them. They had scattered on the prairie and were grazing upon the withered grass. Now they were rounded up into a compact herd. Being chiefly gentle animals stolen from farmers, the best were roped for fresh mounts, and the tired animals ridden in the long chase were turned loose to rest.

As the scouts were making preparations to return with the horses they had recovered, they heard the deep, distinct baying of Jess Warden's dog that had been brought along to trail the Indians but that in the excitement of the running fight with the Comanches had been forgotten.

"That's your dog, Jess," said Sam Henry.

"What do you reckon he's treed?" asked Dick Moreland.

"Warden, don't you hear your hound?" asked George Arnett. Warden was silent for awhile, studying the voice of the hound.

At last he spoke. "That's old Pedro, George, and you

86

must have hit that redskin pretty hard, the one that dropped off his horse."

"Well, let's go to him," said Captain Arnett. Jess Warden led the way, and all hands followed. A run of about a mile, for the most part down a steep, rocky branch toward the recent battlefield, brought them close to the baying of the hound. It came from a dense shin-oak thicket, and they must dismount and crawl on the enemy, who might still be capable of a desperate resistance.

"Let me go ahead; he is my man," said Arnett.

They all paused out of deference to their leader. Upon entering the thicket, he saw just ahead the form of an Indian with his face to the ground, while the faithful hound stood at a respectful distance and barked furiously.

"He may be dead or he may be just possuming," said Arnett as he drew his six-shooter and advanced. He poked the body with the muzzle of his gun, but it was lifeless. "He's dead, all right. Come on and scalp him, Sam; you're good at that job."

Sam Henry gave an exhibition of his skill in scalping that would have done credit to a Kiowa chief, and, cutting the bloody scalp into strips, he gave each member of the party a souvenir of the expedition.

As the tired riders returned with the stolen horses, giving the neighborhood a special reason for giving thanks, the Liberty Hill school was about to dismiss for the holiday.

The schoolhouse stood upon a rocky hill overlooking the South San Gabriel Creek, about two miles from the present village. It was Wednesday afternoon, and the morrow was Thanksgiving. Matt Grant, Andrew Cox, and I had to stay in on "partial payments by the Connecticut rule," while Bascomb Davidson, now lieutenant governor of Texas, worked his examples all out and escaped punishment, just as he always escaped defeat in the primary elections. Ollie Spencer was reprimanded severely for getting Bob Bratton into a scrap, while John Miller was severely lectured for removing the clapper from the teacher's bell.

The criminal docket being unusually light that day, the school was dismissed earlier than usual. Before dismissing, however, Professor Julius Caesar Landrum announced Thanksgiving for the morrow and read President Grant's proclamation. Then, after thrashing George Couch for sticking pins in Tandy Bryson, he had the pupils stand while he and his pretty assistant teacher, Miss Mary Henderson of Georgetown, sang his favorite closing melody:

> I would not live always,
> I ask not to stay.

Then, after a benediction, those youngsters not under any special sentence that afternoon gathered their dinner pails, their empty milk bottles, their blue-back spellers, their slates, and their arithmetics and went whooping down the hill, homeward bound.

Camp Meeting on Jenks Branch

———◆———

WHAT WAS an old camp meeting like? To answer that, I shall go back to 1870 and take a glorious morning in August after the wheat is threshed, the fodder stacked, the sheep sheared, the spring calves branded, and the cowboys back from their long drives up the trail.

The grass was good to stake on, and the mules could be hobbled and not run off. The farmers and merchants, lawyers and doctors, preachers and teachers from Georgetown, Bagdad, Liberty Hill, and Round Rock, and the ranchmen from Williamson, Burnet, and Travis counties had taken a vacation, and many of them had camped at the old Jenks Branch Camp Ground.

This was an ideal place for this simple worship of God, a sequestered spot in the solitude of a wilderness. Not a human habitation was in sight, or any fence or other sign of man's design except the camp. But the camp itself was a bustling little city of tents. To the west stood the hills and cedar brakes that grew rougher and rougher until they terminated in the mountains along the Colorado River. To the east was a prairie covered with rich pasturage, with here and there a thicket of young live oaks offering shade and shelter to hundreds of browsing cattle.

On either side north and south of the camp was a rocky ridge with Spanish oaks and now and then a patch of cedar or an agarita bush full of golden berries. Through the camp flowed Jenks Branch, a dry *barranco* until it reached a large pecan tree, at which point there issued from the bank a cold stream of sparkling water. On the right side of this stream stood the arbor made of boughs from the Spanish-oak forest. A narrow strip of woods along the branch was filled with tents, wagons, and carriages.

A group of barefoot boys waded in the branch as it flowed on its course to San Gabriel Creek. How those boys have scattered! One is a banker in Fort Worth, another an eminent jurist in Austin, and another a leading lawyer in Houston. Two are preachers somewhere in northern Texas. One, a teacher, is in Heaven, I know, for he wrote me shortly before he died and said he was going there. He was killed in a terrible accident. We barefoot boys played in the brook until the horn blew for services; then we ran to the arbor.

What an audience was there! Although the country was sparsely settled, three counties could get up a big crowd. Among the people I saw there were giants, not in stature or in fortune but in character. As I look back, I see the Brysons, Snyders, Faubions, Bartons, Millers, Carrothers, Hodges, Grants, Roddys, Walkers, Matthews, and Parks—men whose every heart was a Gibraltar of strength against temptation.

But there were others, too. One was a professional horse hunter who listed strays in a book and hunted the animals for reward. He went from camp ground to camp ground, asking every man if he had seen anything of a bay mare with a blaze face, saddle-marked, with one white forefoot,

90

branded X on her left shoulder, wearing a bell, and followed by a mule colt. There also was the professional liar, who had seen every animal that you could describe, including a white mule with a black side. There, too, was the professional horse thief from near the head of Devil's Hollow, who knew a great deal more about the location of lost animals than he ever would tell.

There were squads of Snyders' cowboys who had just returned from the trails and who would contract to drive any size herd of any sort of animals from anywhere to anywhere and ride any quadruped that wore hair for thirty dollars and chuck per month. There was also a big Texas Ranger, Captain Jeff Maltby's top sergeant, Andy Mather, home on furlough from the Indian range where he had fought in a battle with the Comanches a few weeks before and had slain the chief with his own hands. The headstall of his bridle was decorated with bits of the chief's scalp. The long black hair from the ghastly trophy hung over the back of the throat latch. The bridle reins were made of human hide flayed from the back of the distinguished savage, twisted thongs of the same material were buttoned around his horse's neck to be used as a hobble.

He tied his horse with pride in a conspicuous place and twisted his long black mustache as he darted glances from his eagle eye at a group of pretty Georgetown girls under the arbor and sat down on a rude bench.

One man with a thin, swarthy visage sat away from the throng. He was a murderer, and everybody knew it. Long incarceration in the Georgetown jail had not bleached the shadows from his face. He had been tried, convicted, granted a new trial, and admitted to bail, and now he was out of jail.

The women were as different in appearance as the men.

91

They were of all types, from the wife of the rich cattle baron with her expensive gown and forty-dollar millinery to the stout, sun-tanned mountain woman in plain cotton plaids fashioned after her grandmother's wedding dress and sunbonnet to match, but with a face beaming with sympathy, purity, and dignity that made every gentleman treat her as a queen.

The preacher rose and said, "Stand and sing, without tuning, 'A Charge to Keep I Have.'" Brother Goodson Bryson pitched the tune, a few others joined in, and then the song spread like contagion through that vast audience. The men and women and children sang. Now the cowboys joined in, and the big Ranger fell in line with a voice that seemed to send the melody above the pecan trees. On the second stanza the song broke out in the camp. The lemonade man broke out down by the spring and the women busy at cooking sang over their campfires until at last the whole valley seemed filled with the song that rose higher and higher and rolled away in ever-widening waves toward Heaven.

A deep pause followed. Then the preacher said, "Let us pray." His prayer seemed to bare every secret in every breast, and at every pause there was a deep chorus of "Amens!"

Then Josiah Whipple, the matchless orator, preached on restitution, reconciliation, and the Judgment. As he handled restitution in his inimitable style, the tall horse thief seemed alarmed. His secret was out. He had had many narrow escapes. Two horses had been shot from under him as he escaped from avenging mobs. Five times he had been tried in three counties for theft. He had been too shrewd for conviction, but now here was an old preacher who knew all and was telling everybody what he had done.

92

The thief looked about and saw the faces of men he had robbed. They saw his embarrassment. They seemed to read the confession in his face. He would like to run away, but the eyes of the preacher were riveted on him.

When the preacher spoke of reconciliation, the murderer started. "If any man have aught against thee," thundered the preacher. The murderer saw a frightful apparition of his dying victim. He had faced an angry mob at Round Rock with indifference. He had listened to a verdict of guilty as charged at Georgetown and heard a sentence of death pronounced without apparent emotion. But here was a scene he could not face.

Men were running to and fro, falling upon one another's necks, and begging for forgiveness. The preacher paused and was weeping. Before the murderer's eyes a different scene was transpiring. He saw his victim asleep on a pallet in his wagon. He saw by the flickering light of the camp-fire the rugged rocks rising above the gurgling waters of Cluck's Spring.

Now he sees his victim raised upon his elbow with bright arterial blood spurting with quick pulsations from a ghastly wound, and he hears his cry, "Oh, for God's sake, don't stab me again!"

Once more the picture slides, and he sees the limp corpse of his victim after the last cruel thrust with his pocketknife is sent home in the victim's heart. The glassy eyes seem to stare at him.

"First, go to him," comes from the preacher in thunderous tones. But the corpse ever before his eyes seems to say, "It's too late now. We can't be reconciled. When you gave me that last stab, you said, 'Dead men tell no tales.' It comes home to you now. Dead men can be parties to no reconciliation."

93

Unable, perhaps, to face the scene, the murderer arose, walked away, mounted his horse, and rode off, never again to return to the Jenks Branch Camp Ground.

The subject of reconciliation did not startle the big Ranger. He, too, had slain his victim; but he was a Comanche, and he had killed in mortal combat. The Indian had murdered white women and taken their children into cruel captivity. The Ranger had slain in self-defense a savage, and he felt as little remorse as if he had killed a mountain lion or a rattlesnake. He felt less pride in his ghastly trophies, perhaps, but if he had mutilated the dead, public opinion had sanctioned it.

Still the Ranger felt conviction. His concept of right and wrong was not as clear as that of the preacher. But he had been on a spree at Fort Concho, and he had gambled with Mexicans in Laredo, and he was not sure that he was justified in shooting at a cowboy at Fort Sill. Now the preacher spoke of the Judgment until the gentle slopes on either side of the camp ground seemed like overhanging rocks that were about to fall on and overwhelm the audience. The giant Ranger trembled with emotion. He felt a hot tear on his cheek. Would the Georgetown girls see it and laugh at him? No, they, too, were weeping.

When the preacher closed, the audience, led by Goodson Bryson, rose and sang, "I Will Arise and Go to Jesus," while the preacher called for penitents to come and kneel at the mourner's bench. The tall horse thief from the head of Devil's Hollow was the first to fall upon his knees and sob aloud. Other penitents followed, and soon the altar was filled with people under deep conviction. The big Ranger arose, gave the preacher his hand, and returned to his seat. At the close of the song the preacher said, "Brother Snyder, lead us in prayer."

94

Tom Snyder was a large cattle driver. Hundreds of young men were hired by him annually to trail vast herds of cattle from Texas ranches to Wyoming and Montana territories. The Snyder brothers were men of piety, and they cared for the spiritual as well as the temporal needs of their men. So when Mr. Snyder saw a number of his cowboys at the altar, he was almost too full for utterance. When his fervent prayer was finished, there were several professions of conversion, and among them was a young man whose mother was a widow. She was so rejoiced that she could not keep from shouting; she did not try, and nobody else tried to control her. They just let her shout, and it seemed to do her a lot of good.

The next day the professional liar at Burnet said, "Whipple had three hundred conversions at Jenks Branch yesterday." The horse hunter at Bagdad said that he had counted only thirty but that among them was the tall horse thief from the head of Devil's Hollow and that he hoped now that his business of finding lost animals would be much easier.

Late Sunday night a farmer, Noble Bryson, returned home from the camp ground. As he unharnessed his team and was putting up his horses, he heard a familiar whinny. It was old Boston, his best wagon horse, that had been stolen a few days earlier. Now Boston, with his head over the rock fence, was begging for corn. Restitution had been made.

Nebraska Train Robbery

ON THE EVENING of September 18, 1877, the Union Pacific station agent at Big Springs, Nebraska, saw six mounted and heavily armed visitors ride up just twenty minutes before the eastbound passenger train was due. The presence of mounted and armed cowpunchers driving pack horses was nothing unusual in that region and excited no suspicion at first, but when they hastily dismounted, entered the office, and covered the agent with their six-shooters, his hands went up in the air.

"Put that instrument out of commission quick," said the robber chief as he leveled his forty-five Colt at the agent's head. Remonstrance was useless. The agent mumbled something at the wires, detached something, and then pronounced the instrument disabled.

"Not yet," said the robber. "Turn her back. That's it. Take out that relay quick if you love your life. Now give it to me."

Dropping the piece in a sack, the robber glanced at the station clock. "How long before the train's due?" he asked. "Fifteen minutes," was the reply.

"Flag her down for us," said the one with the six-shooter.

"Maybe I can't."

"But you must, or you will be a dead man in just seventeen minutes."

Just then a cowboy rode up and dismounted. As he entered the station, the robbers got the drop on him, and he held up his hands. He was then relieved of his guns, his watch, and the several dollars in his pocket. The cowboy took his fate philosophically. He was a ranch foreman, and his salary soon would replenish his depleted finances. He had no fear of the bandits as long as he obeyed them. They ordered him to sit down in the station, and, as he sat, his attentive ear caught the sound of a familiar voice. It was that of the robber chief talking to the agent.

"Now when the train comes in, you flag it down and give the signal for the express messenger to open his car. Understand?"

"Yes, but suppose he doesn't open up?"

"Then you will be a dead man," said the robber.

The imprisoned cowman said to himself, "That's him. I can't be mistaken. No other living man of his weight has so small a foot. He is in disguise now, but I know him, and my time will come someday."

The train was clearly visible, coming across the plains from Julesburg. "Flag 'er down!" ordered the chief as a white puff of steam rose from the whistle. The brakes were applied, and the train slowed down, its momentum carrying the engine a little past the station. The express car stopped just opposite the waiting party.

"Open 'er up," whispered the robber. At a signal from the agent, the car door began to slide. As soon as the crack was wide enough, the robbers caught the door, slid it wide open, and jumped in. The astonished messenger saw that it would be death to resist.

"Open your box!" ordered the chief, as he presented his forty-five. The messenger opened a small safe, and the robbers helped themselves to about a thousand dollars.

"I have a small consignment today," the messenger apologized.

"We are informed differently," said the bandit leader. "Open that big safe in the corner or you are a dead man. Understand?"

"I can't. That's a through safe. It was locked in Frisco and can't be opened until it reaches its destination. I don't know the combination any more than you do."

"Open it or I will blow your brains out," said another of the gang.

"I can't, but I'll try." But a blow on the head from a big six-shooter sent the messenger reeling to the floor of the car.

"Leave him alone!" shouted one of the robbers called Sam. "This boy told you the truth. If you touch him again, I'll shoot you."

The robbers then pried open a box marked "Axes" and found that it contained $10,000 in twenty-dollar gold coins, fresh from the mint. There were six of the ax boxes, and the whole $60,000 was emptied into sacks provided for that purpose. The guard the robber chief had placed over the train crew still held the train while confederates went through the passengers. At the points of revolvers the unlucky people stood and delivered whatever they had of value.

"Hold up both hands!" ordered the leader to a passenger who elevated only one.

"I have but one hand. I lost the other at Gettysburg," said the veteran.

"How much money do you have?"

"None, sir. Your partner has just robbed me."

"How much did you give up?"

"Seven dollars and fifty cents," said the former soldier.

"Here, take it. We don't want your money," said the robber, handing him back some coins.

One passenger had only fifty cents. "What is your occupation?" asked the chief.

"I run a country newspaper," he replied.

"Then take back a dollar for one year's subscription. Got a watch?"

"Yes," said the journalist. "I have a silver watch."

"Keep it. We don't want any white tickers."

With this joke the robber called off his forces, and the train was allowed to proceed.

During the robbery the cowboy prisoner in the depot made his escape and was well on his way to Julesburg. The train carried the news of the holdup to Ogallala, and from there it was telegraphed to Omaha. There was much excitement about Ogallala as the news spread to the neighboring ranches. Cowboys soon began to drop into town and offer their services for the pursuit of the bandits. Among others, Joel Collins came in and tendered his services. Collins who was known to some of the cattlemen, helped to organize the pursuit. Led by him, a brave band of cowboys scoured the plains for many miles around Big Springs, but they found no trace of the robbers after they left the station.

The next day a stranger stepped off the eastbound passenger train at the Omaha station and asked for the office of the superintendent of the Union Pacific Railway. Finding that the official had gone home, the stranger took a carriage and told the driver to take him to the home of the general superintendent. A servant there said that his master must not be disturbed then and told the visitor to call at the office the next morning.

"Tell him I have important business, and tomorrow will be too late. I must see him this evening."

After this message was delivered, the official said to show the gentleman in at once. After introducing himself to the superintendent, the stranger, who was a cattleman, began:

"You have heard of the Big Springs robbery, I suppose."

"Yes. Can you tell me anything about it?"

"Yes, sir. I was there and contributed what I had to the robbers."

"Have you any clue? Is there any way you know to find out who did the work?"

"I know who led the gang, and that is all I know about it. I knew his voice and his figure. I can't be mistaken."

"Who was he?" asked the official, deeply concerned.

"Joel Collins, a Texas cowboy well known about Julesburg and Ogallala."

"Were you on the train that was held up?"

"No, I came to the station while the robbers were there waiting for the train, and I never suspected anything wrong until they got the drop on me. Then they went through me and made me sit inside the station until the agent was made to flag the train. While waiting there I heard their leader give orders for the agent to flag the train and to signal for the expressman to open his car. The robber was masked, but I recognized his voice and his foot. I'm sure he didn't know me, as it had been a long time since we met before."

The cautious official asked the stranger for references.

Those were easily given, for the official knew all the prominent cattle shippers of that part of the range.

"Just wire Captain John Snyder of Cheyenne. He has charge of the Widow Iliff's ranches at Julesburg, at Pine Bluff, and at Cheyenne. He is from Georgetown, Texas, and he and his brothers, Tom and Dudley Snyder, know every reliable foreman that ever came up the trail."

"That will be all right, but can you give me the name of some reliable man at Ogallala who can work up this case against Collins and his band. You see, he must be a man of courage and deliberation."

"Yes, there is Billy Lynch—Red they call him, on account of his red hair. You can depend on Billy. He knows all the Ogallala boys, and he is the man you want. Red keeps a store in a two-story box house just west from the depot, and his family lives upstairs."

"Well," said the official, "I'll act at once on your suggestion. I'll go out tonight in my special car with the best engine in the Omaha shops. I'll go to Billy Lynch and put him on the scent. In the meantime, you shall not be forgotten. The express company offers $10,000 reward, and the Union Pacific Railroad can be depended upon to do its part. If the information you bring me leads to the capture of the robbers, you shall be substantially remembered. Here is my order for your transportation back to your station."

In a few hours the superintendent of the Union Pacific was flying on his train along the beautiful valley of the Platte for Ogallala. It was a long night run, and it was nearly sunrise when he reached his destination. "Red" was just opening his place of business when he was surprised by a visit from the superintendent. They had met before, and when the official requested a secret audience, it was granted. The men were alone in the back of the store.

"Mr. Lynch, where is Joel Collins?" asked the official.

"Why, I reckon he is here in town. He was here to my store yesterday, buying some provisions."

"Please find out for me as quickly as you can."

Billy Lynch quietly withdrew but returned soon with the information that Joel Collins had left on the preceding evening and had crossed the river at the old Texas cow trail, headed southward. Collins was accompanied by several friends. They drove three pack horses and had a complete camping outfit. They had said they were going to Texas over the old trail.

"Who was with Collins, Billy?"

"Henry Heffridge for one. Sam Bass was another, and there was that fellow the boys call Shorty, another called Dutchy, and then Charley. I don't know their names. Dutchy had a pair of red-topped boots charged to him in my store, and also three seamless grain bags. Joel Collins stood for him, and afterward Collins paid the bill. I see now what you are driving at, Colonel. Joel Collins and his gang robbed the train at Big Springs, and, strange to say, I never suspected them until this moment."

"But, Billy, there were six in the robbery, and you account for only five. Who was the other?"

"I don't know, Colonel, unless it was Jim Berry. Jim was a chum of Collins, and, like Bass and Heffridge, he took an active part in the pursuit. That's what they wanted with the grain sacks, and Dutchy is the man with the red-topped boots at the robbery."

"Now, Billy," said the colonel, confidently, "I want you to get a good company and get right behind those fellows. Take right down the trail until you overtake them, then

102

shadow them. Don't get shot, but spare no money or horse-flesh or telegraphing to keep me posted as to their movements. If they follow the cattle trail, they must cross the Kansas Pacific Railway at or near Buffalo station in Kansas. Remember there will be more money to you in helping to capture these robbers than you will get out of your store in a year. The express company offers a big reward, and the railroad will take care of you if you will help us in this matter."

Billy Lynch was a man of decision. After a moment's reflection, he said, "Yes, Colonel, I'll do the best I can."

A few hours after the official left, there was a splash in the waters of the Platte River in front of Ogallala, right on the old Texas trail. The Mormon truckers had not depleted the flow of the South Platte then, as now, by using its waters to irrigate their potato fields in Colorado, and the river was then a turbid flood nearly a mile wide but shallow and always fordable. Billy Lynch's red hair fairly shone with the fires of dogged determination as his sorrel mare Pigeon bore him across the muddy river to its southern shore. Taking the cattle trail, he rode leisurely southward. Urgent as his mission was, he knew it would not do to show undue haste, for ostensibly he was only going out on an antelope hunt, and fast riding while yet in sight of the station might arouse some unpleasant suspicion as to its purpose.

Night overtook him near the head of Stinking Water Creek, and he dismounted and picketed out his mare. After eating a lunch from his little commissary, he spread his blanket on the grass and was soon asleep. By the peep of dawn he was up and going. He rode until late in the afternoon without seeing a human being. The monotony of the treeless plains was oppressive. There were no herds on the trail this late in the season, and, save an occasional herd of antelope in the distance and now and then a sneaking coyote crouching in the grass by the roadside, there was nothing to relieve the sameness of the prospect. The forests have their solitudes, but there is nothing in the stillness of the woods to compare with the oppressive silence of the Great Plains in the long ago.

A cloud of dust on the southern horizon caused William Lynch to adjust his field glass, that indispensable instrument carried by all cautious plainsmen in early days. As the dust rolled away, he discovered nine moving objects in the dim distance. Now, as their trail made a slight curve, they were seen to better advantage. There seemed to be six horsemen, accompanied by three pack horses. Billy now spurred his mare on rapidly to gain a better view. When he took his glass again, he saw that he had gained rapidly on the party and that they either had not noticed him or were willing for him to come up with them. They must be the robbers, and Billy shuddered at the thought of coming up with them, alone as he was. He never doubted that they, too, had a glass and were watching his movements as he watched theirs. Turning his mare at right angles to the trail, he rode away from it as though indifferent to their presence and went some distance off his route. The distant figures seemed to be sinking out of sight. Billy rejoiced.

"They're going down into the canyon of Frenchman's Creek," he muttered as the group disappeared as though the ground had opened and swallowed them. "Now, Pigeon, for a hard ride," and Billy headed the mare straight for the spot where the travelers had disappeared, and, spurring her in both flanks, he galloped forward. In half an hour he had reached the bank of the canyon. He saw that the trail turned sharply to the left and followed the bottom of the canyon. The fresh horse tracks where the animals had slipped and slid down the side of the canyon were plainly visible. "They will camp in the canyon near the Republican River tonight, and I must crawl on them," said Billy to himself.

Early that night Pigeon was picketed on the open plain near the declivity of the canyon in which the robbers were camped. Billy Lynch crept silently down the side and along the bottom of the canyon until within a few rods of the robbers' camp. Then, taking shelter behind a thicket of wild currant bushes, he crawled as a snake until he was in earshot of the highwaymen. The horses of the robbers were picketed along the flat bottom of the canyon below the camp, and, as the men seemed to feel perfectly secure, there was little danger of their coming toward him. He was safe if he could keep hidden. The bandits were in earshot of him.

"We will have to divide the stuff and separate; we can't travel together any longer. I am in favor of dividing up tonight and traveling by twos. Henry Heffridge and I will keep on down the cow trail. Jim is from Missouri and Dutchy from Pennsylvania, so they can go farther east, while Sam Bass and Charlie had better go farther to the west and keep close to the Rocky Mountains. We must never surrender. Better turn your toes up than surrender.

"Sometimes a fellow gets a chance to swap out. Sometimes they get the draw on him and nab him before he knows it. Then he must keep mum. Mum is the word, understand? We must die with our boots on rather than surrender. If one of us is caught in a trap, he must hang rather than squeal. As soon as me and Henry can get down to the Creek Nation, we will be all right. If Sam and Charlie can make it to the Rockies, they can take care of themselves. If Jim and Dutchy can get over into Missouri, Jim's bunch can take care of them. Now, boys, what I dread is getting off these Kansas plains. Understand?"

Yes, they all understood when their leader talked. The boodle was divided according to that honor said to exist among thieves, and all preparations were made to separate before dawn the next day. "Now, boys, I think we had better take a black oath to fight till we die unless trapped some way and then die before we squeal on anyone. Understand?" Joel Collins proceeded to administer the black oath, each swearing to die rather than surrender or divulge their secrets and all swearing to wreak a terrible vengeance upon any member of the gang who would violate his oath. Sam Bass administered the oath to Collins, and the council of war was over.

A moon would rise, and Billy Lynch thought it best to retire. Stealing his way back to Pigeon, he saddled the mare and was soon riding post haste toward Ogallala. After daylight he went to a ranch near the trail and swapped Pigeon off for a fresh horse, paying boot and allowing himself to be cheated to save time. After riding his new mount down, he was again cheated in a horse swap at the expense of the Union Pacific Railway and pressed on to the Ogallala station. There he rushed into the telegraph office and sent a long wire to the general superintendent of the Union Pacific Railway at Omaha.

From Ogallala to Buffalo station, Kansas, was 265 miles by the old Texas trail, and cow ponies living on grass could hardly make the trip in less time than six days. Federal soldiers from Fort Leavenworth had been stationed at every town on the Kansas Pacific Railway from Kansas to Denver to intercept the fugitive robbers in their flight southward. About a week after the Big Springs holdup, two weary-looking cowpunchers, driving a pack horse, came up to the water tank at the Kansas Pacific depot at Buffalo station and watered their thirsty ponies.

The agent at the depot noticed the strangers and followed them across the street to Thomas' store, where the horsemen stopped and one of them dismounted and entered the store. Passing the pack horse, the agent gave the pack a push with his hand as if to annoy the pony but really to feel the contents. He then entered the store and began a conversation with the stranger. In drawing some change out of his pocket to pay Mr. Thomas for a piece of bacon, the man dropped an old envelope to the floor. Before he could stoop to pick it up, the agent handed it to him, reading the name, Joel Collins, on the back of the letter as he did so. Smiling, the agent said, "This is Mr. Collins, I believe."

"Yes, I think I met you here a year ago," the stranger replied.

"Yes, you went through here with a herd of fine Texas cattle. How did you come out with them?"

"All right. I sold them at Deadwood, Dakota, for a good price, and then I went into the mining business and struck it rich. But I got tired of it all and sold out for money enough to do me the rest of my days, and I am going back home."

"Yes," said the agent, "I get homesick, too, sometimes. I expect to go home next winter."

The traveler was now through with his purchases and, nodding good-by, he and his companion rode away down the old trail. The soldiers stationed at Buffalo to watch for the robbers had taken no notice of the cowpunchers. When the agent told them one was Joel Collins and that their pack horse was laden with specie, all was excitement in their camp. As soon as regulars can do anything in their machine-like way, they saddled their horses, mounted, and were bouncing up and down in their "muley" saddles in hot pursuit of the bandits.

Several hours later the regulars returned with the two dead robbers tied across their saddles. Just how it happened will perhaps never be known. Soldiers gave conflicting reports of the meeting, but the official report said that the robbers offered resistance and were shot to pieces by the troops. In their pack was found twenty thousand dollars in twenty-dollar gold pieces dated 1877. They had a quantity of jewelry and watches taken, it was supposed, from the passengers at Big Springs. One of the dead robbers was identified as Joel Collins by the Kansas Pacific agent. The other was not known at Buffalo. Both bodies were held as long as decency would permit on the plains then, and hundreds of people from far and near came to Buffalo to see the dead bandits.

At last it became necessary to bury the dead, and it was announced that no one else would be allowed to see the bodies. After the coffins were closed, some people from a distance across the plains arrived and asked to see the bodies. Their request was at first refused, but one woman in the party pleaded so earnestly that the officer in charge relented and had the coffins opened again. They passed the coffin of Collins with indifference, but when they came to the other, the woman shrieked, "That's him! That's Henry, my husband!"

She stated that his name was Henry Heffridge and that she had married him when almost a stranger. Later she found that he had other names and that sometimes he went by the name of Potter. He had long ago deserted her, and when she heard of the killing of the robbers, she felt an irresistible desire to see the bodies. She then described two tattooed figures on the ankles of her husband, by which the remains were fully identified.

A few weeks later a farmer was standing in a bank in a Missouri town when a stranger stepped in and introduced himself as James Berry, who had been in the West for some time and had now returned, rich from his profits in mining in the Deadwood district. The cashier was glad to see Mr. Berry and to hear of his good fortune. Mr. Berry then deposited some money in the bank and went out to make some purchases for his "home folks" and to hire a team to take him out of town. The farmer recognized him and seemed to meditate for awhile on Jim's sudden riches. Then, stepping up to the cashier, he asked if Berry had made a deposit. Being answered in the affirmative, he asked, "How much?"

"Oh, I should not tell you, but a good sum."

"Any twenty-dollar gold pieces of 1877?"

"Here, look at it," said the cashier, scattering some gold coins on the counter.

"All twenties of 1877," muttered the farmer as he stepped out to look for the sheriff. Before he found an officer, the suspect had hired a rig and left town. Berry told the liveryman he would bring the rig back or send it in the next morning. The officer decided to wait and see what his next move would be. The next morning a boy brought the team in. He was detained while officers went after the suspect. The latter suspected trouble as soon as he saw the officers and tried to escape. He was surrounded in a pasture near the house and mortally wounded while resisting arrest. All efforts to get the dying man to inform on his accomplices were unsuccessful. He died true to his black oath.

During the spring of 1878 the Dallas section of northern Texas was terrorized by a gang of highwaymen, who robbed four trains, and it was currently believed that Sam Bass was at the head of the gang. The governor put the Texas Rangers on the track of the outlaws, one of whom they killed. Another, Jim Murphy, was captured but was released on a straw bond when he promised to rejoin the band and betray Bass.

After rejoining the gang, Murphy fell under the suspicion of one of the robbers, Frank Jackson, who watched him closely. Now the gang, in the expression of Bass, needed more "yaller boys," or twenty-dollar gold coins. So they formed a bold design to rob a Waco bank. Bass, Seaborn Barnes, Jackson, and Murphy went to Waco to look over the situation. In a room in a hotel in Waco, Murphy feigned sleep while the others discussed the outlook. Jackson's suspicions were aroused again, and he said, "Sam, Jim is a traitor. I'm going to kill him right here."

Bass caught the pistol leveled at Murphy and said, "Don't kill him, Frank. Let him sleep. But what do you think now of this Waco haul?"

Jackson favored it, and so did Barnes, but Bass demurred. He said that it would be easy to rob the bank but hard to escape from a place like Waco. The country was too open and too thickly settled. There were too many fences. They must have more "yaller boys," it was true, but they should hunt some easier game. He called Murphy. Jim raised up, rubbed his eyes, and said innocently, "What is it, Sam?"

"Jim," said Sam, "what do you think about drawing on the Waco bank for some expense money?"

"Don't like it, Sam. Too many fences about here—too much prairie country. I'm afraid we can't get away from here. It's too far to any mountains or brush. But, Sam, I know a good place to make a haul. It's Round Rock, a little

110

station on the I. & G. N., that new railroad through Williamson County. All the freighters from Brownwood, San Saba, Lampasas, and Fort Concho go there now instead of Austin. It's a dandy little town, and the bank there handles scads of money. Then it's easy to get away from there. The timber on the head of Brushy Creek comes down close to town, and in the hills on the Sandy the shin oaks are so thick that you can't cuss a cat through them."

"Boys, Jim is right. I know that place, and it's easy to get away from. The Williamson County Bank of Round Rock handles a world of money. What do you all say?"

Whatever Sam suggested was agreed on. Soon the band was mounted and on the road to Round Rock. As soon as they were out of town, Bass and Jackson had a private talk. Then Sam rode up to Jim and said, "Jim, Frank is afraid of you, and I kept him from killing you at Waco, while you were asleep. Now, to quiet Frank, you give me your six-shooter and carry no arms but cook for the outfit."

"All right, Sam, I'll do whatever you say. You know I'm all right, but, to satisfy Frank, you can take my gun and keep it until after the next haul."

"Now, Jim," said the chief, "you must never leave me for a minute. If you do, Frank will shoot you sure. You are cook and must stay at camp. Understand?"

Jim agreed to everything, and they proceeded on the Belton road. At Belton, Sam sent Jim into town to get a five-dollar bill changed, and while there, Jim mailed warnings to Sheriff William C. Everheart of Grayson County and Walter Johnson, deputy United States marshal. Later, from Georgetown, Jim sent a warning to Major John B. Jones of Austin, who commanded the Texas Rangers. Jones sent on horseback to Round Rock three Rangers, one of whom was Dick Ware, afterward United States district marshal of West Texas. The major followed them by train.

On the afternoon of Friday, July 19, three strangers rode from their camp into the "new town" of Round Rock, as that part of the place near the depot was called. Dismounting, they strode over to a store, with saddlebags on their arms. Barnes and Jackson carried guns in their saddlebags, but Bass wore his in a belt, partially concealed by his coat. His gun did not escape the vigilant eye of A. W. (Kige) Grimes, deputy sheriff. Grimes followed the strangers to the store and, walking up to Bass, said, "My friend, aren't you carrying a pistol?"

"Yes," said Bass, who seemed to realize that the game was up, "I have a gun."

"Have you any legal authority to carry it?" asked the officer.

"Yes, do you want to see my authority?" said Bass.

"Yes," said Grimes, "I would."

"Then here it is," said the robber chief as he quickly drew his gun and shot the deputy dead in his tracks. The robbers then bolted for the door to escape, but Major Jones and the Rangers were upon them, and a desperate street battle followed. At the first shot from the Rangers, Barnes fell dead only a few feet from the body of Grimes. Sam Bass ran to the fallen robber and took his saddlebags. Then he and Jackson ran for their horses, firing back at the Rangers as they ran. Bass was wounded in the right wrist and dropped his pistol, but he drew another with his left hand and continued to fire until a shot from the gun of Dick Ware, it is said, pierced his body just as he reached his horse.

Calling to Jackson, he said. "Frank, I'm shot and can't mount my horse." Jackson caught him and, lifting him bodily from the ground, placed him in the saddle. Then, shouting at his own horse, he caught that of Bass by the bridle rein and dashed out through Old Round Rock and into the woods beyond Brushy Creek and made his escape. Once out of sight of the Rangers, he hid the wounded Bass in a pasture of Dudley Snyder and, taking the saddlebags of Barnes, raced off.

The next day Sam Bass was found in a dying condition and was carried back to Round Rock by Milt Taylor, a deputy sheriff of Williamson County. He lived for another day, retaining consciousness to the last and refusing to divulge any of the secrets of his gang. He admitted his part in the Big Springs robbery but refused to give any information about "Charlie" or "Dutchy," the surviving members of the Big Springs gang.

Thus, on July 21, 1878, his twenty-seventh birthday, Sam died within a year of the great express and train robbery at Big Springs, Nebraska. He was the fourth of the six to die, and all four were true to their black oath.

Bibliography

Manuscripts

Fletcher, Roddy W., Biographical sketch of his father, Baylis John Fletcher.

Snyder, Dudley Hiram and John W., Papers, University of Texas Library.

Snyder, Thomas S., Recollections, as told to J. Evetts Haley in an interview, Dallas, Texas, November 7, 1933. Transcript of interview lent by Mrs. Susie Snyder Pace of Dallas, a daughter of Thomas S. Snyder.

Public Records

Victoria, Texas, Mark and Brand Book, office of the County Clerk of Victoria County, entries for 1879.

Newspapers

Dallas Morning News, March 1, 1934.

Ford County Globe, Dodge City, Kansas, July 1, 8, 15, 1879.

Dodge City Times, July 5, 12, 1879.

Fort Worth Democrat, April, May, 1879.

Bibliography

Books

Bryson, J. Gordon. *Shin Oak Ridge*. Bastrop, Texas, J. Gordon Bryson, 1963.

Clay, John. *My Life on the Range*. Chicago, privately printed, 1924. New ed., Norman, University of Oklahoma Press, 1962.

Dobie, J. Frank. *The Longhorns*. Boston, Little, Brown and Company, 1941.

Gard, Wayne. *Sam Bass*. Boston, Houghton Mifflin Company, 1936.

————. *The Chisholm Trail*. Norman, University of Oklahoma Press, 1954.

————. *The Great Buffalo Hunt*. New York, Alfred A. Knopf, 1959.

Hunter, J. Marvin, ed. *The Trail Drivers of Texas*. Nashville, Cokesbury Press, Vol. I, 1920, Vol. II, 1923. 2nd edition, revised, two volumes in one, 1925.

McCoy, Joseph G. *Historic Sketches of the Cattle Trade of the West and Southwest*. Kansas City, Ramsey, Millet and Hudson, 1874.

THE WESTERN FRONTIER LIBRARY, of which *Up the Trail in '79* is Number 37, was started in 1953 by the University of Oklahoma Press. It is designed to introduce today's readers to the exciting events of our frontier past and to some of the memorable writings about them. The following list is complete as of the date of publication of this volume:

1. Prof. Thomas J. Dimsdale. *The Vigilantes of Montana.* With an introduction by E. DeGolyer.
2. A. S. Mercer. *The Banditti of the Plains.* With a foreword by William H. Kittrell.
3. Pat F. Garrett. *The Authentic Life of Billy, the Kid.* With an introduction by Jeff C. Dykes.
4. Yellow Bird (John Rollin Ridge). *The Life and Adventures of Joaquín Murieta.* With an introduction by Joseph Henry Jackson.
5. Lewis H. Garrard. *Wah-to-yah and the Taos Trail.* With an introduction by A. B. Guthrie, Jr.
6. Charles L. Martin. *A Sketch of Sam Bass, the Bandit.* With an introduction by Ramon F. Adams.
7. Washington Irving. *A Tour on the Prairies.* With an introduction by John Francis McDermott.
8. *X. Beidler: Vigilante.* Edited by Helen Fitzgerald Sanders in collaboration with William H. Bertsche, Jr. With a foreword by A. B. Guthrie, Jr.
9. Nelson Lee. *Three Years Among the Comanches.* With an introduction by Walter Prescott Webb.
10. *The Great Diamond Hoax and Other Stirring Incidents in the Life of Asbury Harpending.* With a foreword by Glen Dawson.
11. *Hands Up; or, Twenty Years of Detective Life in the*

117

118